The World's Greatest Ski Holidays

ELIZABETH
HUSSEY

PROTEUS
London and New York

CONTENTS

The World's Greatest Ski Holidays

Acknowledgements

Ski maps have been kindly provided by: Swiss, Austrian, Italian, French, Australian, New Zealand and Scottish tourist and travel services; by Thomson Holidays, Neilson Travel, Enterprise, Supertravel and Ski Holidays Scotland; and by the resorts.

**PROTEUS BOOKS is an imprint of
The Proteus Publishing Group**

United States
PROTEUS PUBLISHING CO., INC.
733 Third Avenue, New York, N.Y. 10017

distributed by:
THE SCRIBNER BOOK COMPANIES, INC.
597, Fifth Avenue, New York, N.Y. 10017

United Kingdom
PROTEUS (PUBLISHING) LIMITED
Bremar House, Sale Place, London, W2 1PT

ISBN 0 86276 021 6 (p/b)
      0 86276 028 3 (h/b)

First published in 1982

© 1982 Proteus Publishing Group

Design by Zena Flax Associates
Series Editor Jemima Kallas

Printed by Printer Industria Grafica sa,
Barcelona, Spain
D.L.B. 26784 – 1982.

Preface

This is an intimate book written by an expert. Elisabeth Hussey has visited the ski areas selected here, and mingles a factual rundown on lifts, skipasses and accommodation, with glances at ski technique, equipment and, above all, personal experience, so that each resort becomes unique and each one is capable of making a great ski vacation.

Utah's famous powder snow whirls in the face and throat of the reader; the skier visits a small Austrian bedroom in a ski area, with its crisp, darned bed linen and holy picture over the basin; or lands on a glacier in the spurting snow whipped up by the helicopter's blades. The driver is vividly transported onto icy roads where both the handbrake and the windscreen wipers have frozen, and is told what to do.

What makes a great ski holiday is a matter of taste: vertical drops or gentle crosscountry pistes; an après ski of discos, or good eating, or the intimacy of a touring hut in Lapland's wastes; the choice of a purpose-built resort or the charm of an older center. Both would-be skiers or those who have skied but want to extend their range will find this book the right guide.

Jemima Kallas
Editor

Introduction

Skiing offers vacations for everyone, from infants to grandfathers, even though it is associated with the young and lively. In its variety, it actually attracts both crowdlovers and hermits, racers and ramblers. For some its essence is a swift dash down a busy piste with a group of friends while music pours out of loudspeakers; for others it can be a steady jog deep in the woods where the only sounds are the swish of skis along the tracks, the occasional scrabble of a squirrel or the song of a bird.

The very idea of a ski holiday conjures the sparkle of sunshine on snow, the challenge of the elements, the intoxicating air of the mountains. Blue skies, bright clothes, tanned skin, plenty of exercise, beautiful, sometimes awesome surroundings by day followed by evenings spent in a disco shaking to the vibrations of the latest rock music. This is the essence of a great ski holiday.

Even some of those who ski every year know only one kind of ski holiday; they return to the same resort with the same tour operator year after year. Few realise the enormous variety offered by the mountains, so this book describes some of the greatest ski vacations to be found all over the world. Even the most conservative skiers may come to realise that they are missing something which is just waiting to be enjoyed. A new dimension can be added to their holiday.

Most vacations start with planning where to stay. Hotels vary from five-star luxury to cheap bed and breakfast, but here choice usually depends upon the amount of money there is to spend. Some people may not know that they can also choose to stay in a chalet run by chalet girls, who combine the virtues of super cooks, cleaners, hostesses, mines of information about the resort and providers of a comfortable home background. Chalet holidays are less formal and more friendly than hotels and they offer advantages like afternoon tea and free wine. Other people may prefer to do their own catering and then there is the choice of chalet or apartment; renting, buying outright or buying on the new system of time-sharing.

Beginners need a good ski school; gentle nursery slopes which are within easy reach of their hotel; plenty of atmosphere both in the village streets and within the hotels at night. There is little point in their going to the high-altitude complexes with enormous ski areas, for they pay disproportionately for everything (prices tend to rise with altitude in the mountains) and cannot use the full scope of the expensive liftpasses. Altitude can be heady for the fit and expert but it can also stop the unfit from sleeping and cause beginners to puff and pant as they fall about and struggle to get up again.

As skiers improve, so they need more scope; a greater variety of slopes to explore; more lifts to take them up higher or further from their resort; steeper gradients to challenge their daring. For the expert there is the ultimate in ski experience, heliskiing. Only the fit and competent should try this kind of trip, for the flights up by helicopter into remote areas of mountain are followed by very long descents through areas untroubled by other skiers.

Some slopes are reached not by helicopter but by laborious uphill trek by skiers carrying with them all they need for survival in the way of food and drink. They spend the nights in huts built by touring clubs with basic accommodation, which often means rolling up in a blanket and lying on long, mattressed shelves.

Quite another kind of touring is done by those who use the long thin light skis, developed by the Scandinavians when they used them as the only way to get about in winter time. This kind of crosscountry skiing is usually done along trails cut through the trees. It is invigorating and sweeps away the stress of days spent during the rest of the year behind a desk or in a car.

There are vacations which are specially suited to children – or to families who want their children to be happy and well cared for while they enjoy the freedom to ski and go out to dinner; a holiday from looking after the children but with them always close, rather than left at home. Many resorts now specialize in looking after children and this can make a true vacation for parents.

Other families want a mixed vacation; where one of them can enjoy a town holiday while the other enjoys the slopes. The entertainments and sophistication of big cities often lie close to excellent slopes and no one need feel they have been cut off in a remote village when they are surrounded by the stimulation of shops, cinemas, opera, good restaurants and museums.

Even winter is not essential any longer for winter sports, for there are now resorts high enough to ski all through the year. Summer skiing has its own quality; early morning starts to benefit from the best snow conditions; the high altitudes with energetic piste skiing through the morning; then down to the valley to spend a long afternoon by the swimming pool or to use up surplus energy in tennis, horseriding or walking.

The variety of ski resorts is as great as the variety of slopes. The big rich traditional wintersport resorts offer far more than just skiing. In the twenties and thirties, villages started to adapt themselves to skiers; then resorts such as Courchevel and Sestriere were built from the start with skiers in mind. In the 1960s, the French developed a new kind of resort built high in the mountains where the snow was certain to fall in the winter and where the architecture was perfectly adapted to the needs of skiers.

Not everyone wants this purpose-built modern atmosphere for their vacation. The traditional village with old chalets and a central spired church, pubs and bars to drink in of an evening, a bowling alley perhaps and the occasional glimpse of cattle patiently awaiting the change of seasons in their dark midwinter sheds, offers another dimension to skiers. Here there is more chance to see a foreign way of life; the après-ski entertainment often takes the form of folklore evenings.

We have spent more pages describing Europe and the Alps than anywhere else in the world because it was in the European Alps that skiing was first developed as a sport. Now tourism has spread rapidly round the world. The American Rockies have been developed more recently and offer the very best snow in the world, so light and powdery that the skier has to keep his mouth shut as he descends through the rippling layers, lest it get into the lungs. American capital, American knowhow and American enthusiasm has produced truly great resorts with all the comfort and variety for which the country is noted.

Around the world skiing has developed unevenly. The Andes are superb and grand but communications make holidaying there difficult except for those living in Santiago or Buenos Aires. In Australia the crowds flock to Thredbo or Perisher and much development is being done. In Britain, Scotland produced excellent slopes with internationally recognized race courses, good lifts and a great deal of enthusiasm.

All over the world skiers are battling with conservationists to develop more areas where they can enjoy their sport. One thing is sure: skiing will continue to provide great vacations in hundreds of different ways. We hope this book will give skiers the chance to get the best out of their pilgrimage to the mountains.

WHERE TO STAY

Chalet parties

*S*urely the most relaxed and comfortable *background to a ski holiday is the staffed chalet. This European custom offers the comforts of home without the housework; the benefits of a hotel without the intrusion of strangers.*

Tour operators offer chalets and apartments for as few as six or as many as 30 people. Chalet girls who look after them during the season keep them tidy, make beds and provide breakfast, tea and supper.

Some chalets or apartments can be taken over entirely by a family or a group of friends. There are often good discounts when a big chalet is booked outright by a group, so that the tour operator deals with just one organizer rather than each person separately. The organizer, of course, takes the risk of someone dropping out at the last moment and this occasionally leads to agonized pleas in the small advertisements of newspapers for a replacement to make up numbers.

If individual bookings are made the tour operator will usually try to slot people into groups that suit them. Some chalets are reserved for families with children, where the younger ones can play as noisily as they like without bothering anyone and dinner can be served early to suit them. Chalet girls will often babymind for the evening, so that parents can go out on the town without worrying about their children.

Other chalets are kept exclusively for 17–35 year olds who have their own parties of an evening. Some brochures suggest bringing out favorite tapes so that the living room can turn into a nightclub after dinner without nightclub prices. Another suggestion is that duty free drink should be bought at the international airports en route for chalet consumption. Unlike hotels, which need to make profits in their bars, chalets will usually supply tonics, fruit juices and other mixes at supermarket prices to go with their guests' own alcohol.

Not all chalets are exclusive to one grouping of people. Because accommodation is difficult to find in many resorts, the operators are turning more and more to small hotels which they run as big chalets with a mixture of guests. These have the advantage that if there is someone obnoxious in the party there is enough room for people to keep away. Also, the bigger the chalet, the more likely it is to cater for single people with single rooms.

Food plays an important part in chalet life. Most chalet girls are superb cooks. No continental breakfast or coffee and rolls here, sitting sadly alone on the breakfast table. Instead, fruit juices, eggs and porridge are added to send the skier off to the slopes. Afternoon tea is a special meal with steaming hot chocolate and great pots of tea together with home made cakes and biscuits. Chalet dwellers are encouraged to bring their friends back to tea – if only to show them what they are missing, so they book into a chalet next time.

The evening meal is a new experience each night. Clothes may be informal but dinner consists of three courses at least, beautifully prepared and presented. Wine and coffee are included without extra charge.

Chalet girls are chosen for their personality as well as their cooking ability. Because they are in a resort for a whole season and usually arrive in the mountains early in December to prepare for their guests, they get to know their resorts well. They are mines of useful information about the best areas for skiing in the morning or the afternoon; the best ski hire shops; the best local liftpass to suit the beginner or the expert skier. They even – by force of circumstances – get to know the resort's electricians, carpenters, plumbers and, of course, ski instructors. They can tell which night clubs are good value and which are expensive; also which doctors are the most reliable. As altitude tends to heighten emotions, they need to be level headed and, above all, to care about the people they are looking after.

The big operators are the safest bet when booking a chalet holiday as they have resources to fall back on if things go wrong in the mountains. Even chalet girls can break legs while skiing and in a chalet run by one girl this could mean a disastrous vacation. A good back-up service is needed to install a replacement. The bigger hotel-cum-chalets are, of course, run by as many as four or five girls, so such problems are not so serious. In little chalets, guests are asked to take one evening meal a week out, to allow the girl an evening off but with the big chalets this too is unnecessary.

Water is often a problem in a ski resort, especially in high altitude villages where natural springs freeze up in winter, so in some chalets the number of baths or lavatories can be limited. It is a point to watch when booking.

Chalet life is addictive. Once having spent a vacation with such a comfortable, relaxed and work-free background, it is difficult to think of returning to the more formal hotel or coping with shopping and housework in a holiday apartment. For those who go on holiday alone, the chalet supplies a group of acquaintances with whom to ski by day and après-ski by night. For a set of friends it offers a constant houseparty.

There is something about spending a long day out on the slopes, battling with the mountains and the snow and knowing that a delicious tea is being prepared in a comfortable home, that is very reassuring.

Self catering holidays

Many skiers prefer to enjoy familiar comforts when they come off the slopes and like to make their holiday base a home from home, a place where there are no time limits, no waiting for breakfast or having to be back by eight for dinner. Lunches can be made up as different picnics each day or simply eaten out at mountain restaurants. There is no restaurant surcharge on wine bought at the local shop for dinner. Housework is minimal in the dust-free atmosphere. Best of all, friends can be invited round at any time, to have a drink by the fire perhaps, talk of the events of the day and plan the next day's skiing.

Uto Ring
Apartments,
Val d'Isere

There are several ways of finding a holiday home: renting an apartment, condominium or chalet for a vacation, buying one outright or taking shares in a multi-ownership system which gives a home for a particular fortnight of each year.

Renting an apartment or chalet is easy and has the advantage that a different resort can be tried each year. Companies such as Swiss Chalets-Interhome have thousands on offer. It is just a case of choosing the size, date and location which suits the family or group of friends best.

Yet some of the feeling of a home from home is lost in rented accommodation. Buying an apartment, offers the opportunity to get to know an area, the neighbors and the shops. Apartment ownership also allows the owners to decorate and furnish inside as they like, provided the outside is not touched. Buying a condominium, where the owner takes a share in the building, gives a say in such things as the exterior decoration, party staircases, elevators and surrounding paths.

One of the great advantages of buying an apartment or condominium in a ski area is that the management always see that everything is ready when the owner arrives. Paths are swept, electricity and water are switched on; even the store cupboard and deep freeze are sometimes stocked. Privately-owned chalets may take more trouble to open up but they are particularly desirable for those who want the use of the accommodation in summer as well as winter (provided someone is prepared to keep the garden tidy). Many resorts have rich summer facilities: walking, swimming, horse riding, river-rafting, climbing, tennis and, if the resort is high enough, even summer skiing.

Buying a second home outright is naturally expensive and the great alternative now is 'multi ownership', 'time sharing' or 'time ownership'. With this system, just a particular week or two weeks of every year is bought – say the last week of December and the first in January, which would be high season in the Alps; or the two weeks after that, which would be low season. Low season ownership prices drop to $1000 (£500) outright for a week in perpetuity for an apartment, plus a small weekly maintenance cost. The United States and France were the first countries to sort out good rules for time sharing. Now it has spread all over the world but the system works best where there is stable local government and good central organization.

The idea is to purchase a freehold share in, for example, a block of apartments, which entitles the shareholder to use a specific apartment for a specific period in the year. Many of the buildings are luxuriously equipped with heated pools, saunas and jacuzzis, plus tennis courts and golf courses for the summer, available free of charge to the shareholders. Reductions on lift-tickets and ski hire often go with these arrangements, and even laundry and babyminding often come free in French resorts. A central management deals with the upkeep of the building and its surroundings, the cleaning and maintenance of the apartments between owners and general administration.

The management will help to let a shareholder's apartment if it is not wanted by the owners for their particular period, and many of the companies operate an exchange allowing owners to trade their time share in their apartment one year for one in another resort. Some of the better-known multi-ownership companies have properties all over the world so that Hawaii, Acapulco or a Scottish castle may be exchanged for a ski resort. Grass skirts, or grouse moors may seem a long way from ski slopes but it gives owners the freedom to get away from skiing every now and then.

Like many investments, owning a home can be a gamble. Whether or not a resort prospers depends on how it is managed; on the building of local lifts and other property; and perhaps on the luck of the weather which may leave the slopes short of snow for a couple of difficult years. Sometimes laws are passed which affect prices. For some years the Swiss made it difficult for foreigners to buy land, causing a slump in property values and preventing some resorts from expanding. Now, fortunately, the law has been changed. In contrast Aspen, in Colorado, has recently forbidden building, and property values have risen sky high.

A point to watch is the distance of the apartment from the shops as well as how far it is to the slopes. It is no fun struggling up a narrow snowy path with a bag full of provisions. Happily, many of the modern blocks have supermarkets in the apartment buildings, so that it is not even necessary to put on coat and boots before going out to buy food.

Every kind of restaurant can be found in ski resorts and people who are doing their own cooking can escape it to try local delicacies without the guilty feeling that a hotel meal has been prepared for them and paid for. Yet somehow cooking is not such a chore when the ingredients are so varied, with all the local specialities like wines and cheeses, game and honey. If there are finicky young children, self catering has the additional advantage that whatever suits the children can be brought from home.

The best way to test out the self catering potential of a resort is to visit it first on a package tour, so as to find out how easy it is to buy and cook food in a particular resort, how friendly the local people are, and whether the slopes are right for the family. If the place is good, the next step is to go to the tourist office, which has lists of apartments and chalets to buy, and names of companies offering condominiums or time sharing schemes.

Hotel holidays

A hotel may be just a place to eat in, sleep and keep belongings, or its atmosphere may change the whole flavor of a vacation. The best hotels – and they may be pensions or palaces – are permeated with the grandeur of their setting, even when darkness falls and drawn curtains keep out the views of mountains and forests.

Unlike self-catering holidays, hotels give complete freedom from house cleaning and cooking. Unlike chalet holidays, they offer complete privacy – no risk of sharing a bedroom or eating with strangers. Lounges and bars allow people to meet if they feel like it; otherwise those who book into hotels can keep themselves to themselves.

Typical of the cheapest form of accommodation is the Austrian home offering bed and breakfast to a half dozen guests. The father of the family may have a job as ski instructor, carpenter or lift attendant. Mother welcomes the visitors and shows them the small cluttered room, wash basin in the corner, duvet-covered bed sagging with the weight of many previous sleepers. There is a chair, a wooden cupboard with a few bent coathangers and a holy picture over the bed. The well-polished, wood floor creaks underfoot; towels and bed linen are well-washed and darned.

In the morning, at breakfast, other guests exchange *Guten Tag* as they extract their tablenapkins from the white paper envelopes and settle to coffee, fresh rolls and jam. There is a warm and relaxed welcome in these village homes. In spite of spending little time indoors, the visitor usually gets to know the family quickly, if only because they are around on the stairs and in the kitchen; the children help with the chores when not at school, and the father gives a hand with the baggage.

Small hotels, which provide supper as well as bed and breakfast, often have the same feeling of family homes. French hotels, for example, are often handed down from generation to generation and grandmother may still be a power behind the scenes long after mother has taken over in the kitchen and father is dealing with the accounts.

Here the room may be more comfortable; a partition in one corner hides a shower and bidet; flower-patterned curtains match the bedspread; a telephone on the bedside table offers the opportunity to order breakfast in bed with croissants still warm from the bakery. A search will reveal a pillow to replace the rolled bolster and sheets and blankets to supplement the duvet.

In the evening Madame will provide a simple meal: soup of the day, veal, chicken or stew, followed by the inevitable choice of cheese, fruit or cream caramel. There is usually a bar or small sitting room where guests can read, chat or play cards.

In complete contrast is the stereotyped hotel now being built in increasing numbers by hotel chains in ski resorts. Found at its best in the United States, the plan is familiar all over the world – and indeed in cities and by ocean shores as well as in the mountains. Everything is predictable. Time-and-motion study has decreed just where reception, elevators, and rooms will be sited. Unlocking the room door, the visitor finds bed, table, chair, cupboards and drawers arranged to a master plan. There is no need to wait for a bathroom – one is attached to every bedroom. Heating is adjustable, sound proofing good.

Unlike in the family-run pensions and small hotels, labor is unobtrusive and kept to a minimum; organization takes over instead. Breakfast tends to be self service, and especially in America consists of a splendid array ranging from muffins and maple syrup to eggs and bacon, with fruit, cereal, buttermilk, tea and coffee. Starting the day with this kind of meal means the skier can get by with just a snack for lunch. It all makes sense when coming back from the slopes to eat a big meal at midday just wastes good skiing time.

Even in these stereotyped surroundings, where atmosphere plays second fiddle to comfort and convenience, the life of the mountains percolates – and through the most unlikely source – the TV set. Many modern resorts operate closed circuit television giving weather reports and news of which runs are in the best condition; whether races or expeditions are planned; and including interviews of local and visiting celebrities.

At the top of every European hotel list are the many-starred palace hotels, nearly always run by the Swiss, whose country has such a great hoteliers tradition and the best catering schools in the world. It is not difficult to think of Swiss families whose hotels are handed down from generation to generation. The Badrutts and Markys of St Moritz; Gredigs at Davos, von Allmens and their cousins von Almens on either side of the Lauterbrunnen valley. All have an organization, welcome and understanding of the needs of travelers which comes from very long experience.

Great hotels have flair and panache. They give their guests the impression that they are staying in a home – albeit a stately one where every luxury is at their fingertips. The service is impeccable and discreet; cleanliness is scrupulous; every meal is a discovery of delicious flavors; the furniture is antique and works of art hang on the walls. Even many of the people staying in these palaces offer a spectacle of princes and personalities. Through the luxury runs the character of the mountains; they retain a rustic charm which sets them above the sometimes clinical comfort of conventional hotels. The stone and wood from the mountain-scape which surrounds them is used to put a protective shell round a luxurious cocoon. Most important of all, the staff seem genuinely anxious that guests should relax and enjoy their holidays.

The problem when booking a ski vacation is to decide which form of hotel to aim for; then how to find it. Hotels and *pensions* exist at every level of cost in most resorts. Tourist offices supply lists, and tour operator brochures often include brightly colored pictures with equally colored descriptions. Success in picking the right accommodation usually entails a good deal of reading between the lines.

If a hotel is said to be conveniently near the slopes, it may be excellent for the first run of the day, but a wearisome trudge back from dinner in the village at night. A central hotel may be opposite a disco which ejects a noisy crowd into the moonlit streets at 2 am. South-facing balconies are lovely in resorts where runs are short and everyone comes back to eat a hotel lunch, but they are a waste of money for those planning to be out on the slopes all day.

Water can still be a problem in some resorts where natural springs freeze up in winter and big demands are made by everyone wanting to bath when they come off the slopes. But modern resorts have big reservoirs. Heated swimming pools, hot tubs and jacuzzis mean fewer people are running baths.

It is easy to draw up a list of priorities, which may range from a spare pillow and a waste paperbasket, to sound insulation from the creaking bedsprings in the next room. Some people find a sauna the essential follow-up to a day on the slopes; others appreciate a turned-down bed with a chocolate bar accompanying the goodnight wishes of the management. But top of everyone's list, whether they are staying in a small room or a fully-equipped suite, is the warmth of welcome which radiates from any good hotel.

SWITZERLAND

Jüngfrau region

Davos · Klosters

Zermatt

Verbier

St Moritz

SWITZERLAND

Jüngfrau region

Mürren   Wengen

Grindelwald

Skizentrum / Centre de ski / Ski centre

Kleine Scheidegg – Männlichen

Mit der Eisenbahn ins Skizentrum
Fahren Sie im «Oberländer»-Sportzug ab Biel, Bern oder mit direkten Schnellzügen ab Basel und Zürich. Sportbillette ab allen grösseren Bahnhöfen.
Generalabonnemente nach Mass erhalten Sie in der Jungfrau-Region.

Dans nos stations de ski par le train...
Train de sports «Oberländer», au départ de Bienne ou Berne. Trains directs au départ de Lausanne, Fribourg ou Neuchâtel. Billets à tarif réduit dans toutes les gares principales. Abonnements généraux «à la carte» dans la Région de la Jungfrau.

By train to the ski centre
Take the direct express trains from Basle, Berne or Zurich to the Jungfrau Region. On arrival, you will be given your «made-to-measure» ski-pass.

JUNGFRAU REGION SKI FACTS
Top station 9,748 ft /
3 mountain railways /
4 cable cars /
Many chairs and drags /
Maximum rise 3,688 ft /

High in the Canadian Bugaboos, range upon range of white peaks stretch away towards the horizon giving an impression of infinite wilderness. Between the chalets of Zermatt, the Matterhorn rises up like a challenge to the sun. Up in the Caucasus the twin peaks of Elbrus seem to ride like a white ship at anchor on the mountain waves around them. Perhaps the most sensational view of all is provided by the Eiger, Monch and Jungfrau seen from Mürren across the great chasm of the Lauterbrunnen valley. Even the makers of the James Bond film *On Her Majesty's Secret Service* could not fake a backdrop as beautiful as that provided for them here when Alpenglow tinged the peaks with crimson and the sky was banded with flame, yellow and green to starry blue above.

The area around the Jungfrau mountain and more particularly the
resorts of Mürren, Wengen and Grindelwald which lie close to it, was
the scene of the 'golden age' of skiing in the twenties and thirties.
During this period skiing ceased to be a matter of crosscountry
transport and became a downhill sport. The first modern slalom was
set on the slopes of Mürren in 1922 by Sir Arnold Lunn, the British ski
pioneer.

Mürren, Wengen and Grindelwald differ greatly and their people
quarrel in a friendly way as might be expected in close resorts. 'They
have nothing to do but pick flowers,' say the Mürreners about Wengen
as they look down when snow is short. 'Nowhere to ski up there,' say
the Wengeners of Mürren. Neither is true.

Mürren is the smallest of the three villages. With only 1,000 beds for
tourists, it lies apart from the other two on a shelf facing East above the
Lauterbrunnen valley. Sheltered and sunny, it consists of two roads
which join at one end by the station and at the other by a skilift. The
lower road is near the edge of a great cliff and the hotels along it are
built out like eyries.

Behind the village the ski slopes run up and down three almost
parallel ridges, the Schiltgrat, the Allmendhubel and the Maulerhubel,
which run roughly East-West, so that every possible orientation of
slope can be found. Enthusiastic offpiste skiers can find an infinite
variety of snow conditions within each day's skiing range. The North
facing powder of the Blümenlucke and the spring snow on Wintertal
Fields are the best of their kind.

Until 1971 the runs were all fairly short but then a great cableway was
built from Stechelberg in the Lauterbrunnen valley up through
Mürren to Birg at 8,760 ft and then by another link up to the Schilthorn
where it culminates at 9,750 ft in the Piz Gloria station with a revolving
restaurant. The runs at the top are not difficult and keep their snow
well into the early summer. There is a challenging run, which cuts
down through a steep gulley – the Kanonenrohr back to Mürren. There
are plenty of steep slopes in Mürren, including the famous Kandahar
face, with aptly named Broody Bump, where skiers pause to look for
the easiest route down.

Recently lifts have been built on the Schiltgrat and on the slopes
below the Maulerhubel ridge which give scope for intermediates and
there is a wide gentle slope by the upper road which makes a
convenient nursery area.

A unique race takes place each January from the Schilthorn at
9,750 ft right down to Lauterbrunnen at 796 ft. Only one or two control
points are put in for the safety of racers, otherwise they choose their
own routes and the snow is not prepared as it is for ordinary downhill
races. Half a century ago, when the race was first run, competitors had
to climb up the night before and stay until dawn in the Schilthornhut.
Now the cablecar carries them up there in minutes.

The race has become so popular that entries now have to be
restricted to around 1,200 people and these are sent off at short
intervals, so that a good competitor will pass many others on the long
way down. It is thrilling to stand on a hogs back ridge opposite the
Kanonenrohr and watch as many as a dozen skiers on the face,

FACTS

Location
The Jungfrau range is in the Berner Oberland region of German-speaking Switzerland, East of Lake Geneva. The Jungfrau itself is 13,642 ft; the ski areas range from the Schilthorn (9,750 ft) to the Lauterbrunnen valley (796 ft). Development began in the 20s and 30s.

Resorts
The villages of Mürren (5,643 ft), Wengen (4,180 ft) and Grindelwald. Skiing to suit all standards. The three resorts share over 28 lifts, including a funicular railway, five cables and seven chair lifts.

Accommodation
1,000 beds in Mürren; 5,000 and 6,000 beds in Wengen and Grindelwald, distributed throughout a variety of hotels.

Activities
Curling, ice hockey, indoor swimming, tobogganing, ski bobbing, spring skiing and touring.

estimating in split seconds just where to get the greatest speed while avoiding other competitors.

Mürren is small because there is no room for it to expand on its shelf. It is run by the Gemeinde, a village council which consists of the local families. They have managed to retain the character of their village, and the old wooden chalets and cowbyres remain. There is no road up to the village, which is reached by an old cog railway from Lauterbrunnen or the new cablecar from Stechelberg, so no cars disturb the peace or clutter the roads. The low ratio of beds to ski lifts means that queues are rare on the lifts.

Small as it is, there is a recognized round of meeting places. The Sunny Bar of the Jungfrau hotel for a pre-lunch drink; Sonnenberg, on a crossroads of pistes for lunch on the mountain; the Bellevue hotel for tea; the Eiger hotel's Tächi Bar before dinner; its Stubli for a fondue and its swimming pool sauna and solarium at any time. Late nights can be spent in the Inferno discotheque under the Palace Sport hotel.

Wengen and Grindelwald lie on the other side of the valley, below the Eiger and Jungfrau. Larger than Mürren, they have 5,000 and 6,000 tourist beds respectively but Wengen also retains its village character by banning cars from its streets.

A railway runs up to Wengen from Lauterbrunnen and continues on via Kleine Scheidegg (where a branch leads off to Eigergletscher and the Jungfraujoch) to Grund and Grindelwald. It then returns to the valley at Zweilutschinen. Skiers use the railway as a jumping off place for many slopes but the whole area between Wengen and Grindelwald is now criss-crossed by tows, chairs, gondolas and two cablecars. One cablecar rises 8,089 ft on the far side of Grindelwald up to Oberjoch.

There are plenty of easy and long intermediate runs in the area. One of the best starts at the top of the Männlichen lift from Wengen and streams comfortably down to Grindelwald, but for those who take two weeks holiday a year and want plenty of runs in beautiful scenery to give them a new route to explore every day, this is an ideal area. It also suits families who are all at different standards, for there are some steep bowls with expressive names like Oh God! Down from the Lauberhorn shoulder into Wengen runs one of the major World Cup races of the season. The first Lauberhorn downhill was run in 1930 and its founder, Ernst Gertsch still lives in Wengen. For any member of the family who has not skied before, there is a broad nursery area right in the center of the village.

Curling is a speciality of the region and there are outdoor curling rinks in Wengen and Mürren. Rather like bowls on ice, it is played by sliding flat bottomed 'stones' across the ice towards a target. In fine weather, great sheets are hung beside the rinks to stop the sun melting the ice. On the rinks curlers huddle round the target area or run furiously along in front of their stones, sweeping a smooth path for it with little brooms.

The villages also provide ice hockey, indoor swimming pools, tobogganing and ski bobbing. A more serious preoccupation is, of course, mountaineering. Kleine Scheidegg is the starting point for climbs of the fearsome Eiger North Face, upon which many a mountaineer has lost his life. The great dark wall rears overhead as skiers stumble light heartedly down the Grindelwald nursery slopes.

The Jungfraujoch railway takes tourists up to a spectacular view at 11,333 ft and they can also visit the ice caves. It also brings ski tourers up to an excellent area for spring skiing. Tours lead over the Aletsch glacier to Riederalp or the Lötschental, or they can go across the Petersgrat and past the Mutthorn hut down into the Lauterbrunnen valley. A guide is, of course, necessary for these are long journeys far away from marked pistes and patrols.

The Jungfrau (Meier)
Swiss National Tourist Office

SWITZERLAND
Davos · Klosters

map *page 28*

All round the world Swiss hoteliers are renowned for the comfort and efficiency of their hotels. Swiss trains run to time; the mail arrives regularly; the lifts do not break down. It is the perfect background for relaxation and one which makes any region in Switzerland one of the great ski vacation areas.

A stranger might be forgiven for not realizing he was in a ski resort when arriving at Davos, even though it lies at 5,118 ft. It is no picturesque village but a solid town of flat roofed hotels and

Ice skating in Davos (*Giger*)
Swiss National Tourist Office

apartments, with busy streets full of excellent shops and cafés where it is tempting to sit and watch the crowds.

The solid German-Swiss influence permeates the town. Its people are traditionally opposed to flights of fashion. In the Canton of Grisons where it lies, cars were banned until 1927 unless drawn by horses, and even today no discotheques are allowed in Davos.

Yet Davos has been a ski resort since the turn of the century when two English brothers named Richardson brought Norwegian skis there and tried them out on the slopes opposite the church, encouraging the local children to copy them and ski for fun. There are five great ski areas surrounding it: Pischa with a lift up to 8,153 ft; Jakobshorn and Bramabuel (8,500 and 8,126); Rinerhorn (8,170) and the Schatzalp-Strela area which now links with the most famous of all, the Weissfluhjoch area, which reaches up to the peak at 9,262 ft as well as leading to the famous Parsenn run.

On the Weissfluhjoch stands the Swiss Avalanche Research Institute. Here a great deal of work has been and is being done on what causes snow to stick to a slope; how the various layers deposited at different temperatures interlock; how potential avalanche slopes can be made safe for skiers and how buried skiers can be rescued. Rescue methods by radio transceivers, avalanche rods and dogs are constantly reassessed. A meteorological station monitors the weather, collects reports and sends out warnings about unsafe areas all over Switzerland. The Parsenndienst, who patrol the slopes, are the most experienced squad in the world.

Davos also has Switzerland's largest skischool; 220 instructors teach on its slopes. They give special classes for children, mini-ski lessons, take tests, teach crosscountry and take classes away from the crowded pistes on day or week-long tours. For, as well as having 75 miles of marked pistes, Davos and Klosters are surrounded by superb touring country which reaches up into the Silvretta group behind Klosters and continues on into the valleys of Austria beyond.

The pistes are very varied. The long, easy descent of the Parsenn is fine for intermediates. Above it, the steeper slopes from the Weissfluhjoch are still manageable and there are the kind of pistes skiers dream about down Dorftalli and the Meierhofer Talli as well as spring snow rambles off to Kublis, Fideris or Jenaz. Yet Strela, whose gondola parallels the Parsenn railway up to the Strelagrat (8,200) is gentle enough to inspire confidence on the first day out on the slopes.

There is quite a different atmosphere on the steeper slopes of the Jakobshorn and Bramabuel, where the mogul fans congregate. Bramabuel does have some wide pistes through thin wood down to Ischalp but ability is needed to come cleanly through the bumps. From the round gondola station on the Jakobshorn (8,500 ft) there is plenty of choice in the runs down to Usser Isch, Clavadeler or the Jatzhorn lift and a fine run far away to Sertig.

Both the Pischa and Rinerhorn lifts give intermediate skiers a chance to spend days exploring areas well within their capabilities.

Klosters, which is just 8 miles away by road and 1,000 ft lower than Davos, is linked to the Parsenn area through the Gotschnagrat lift. Even experts find the fearsome Gotschnawang very steep but the route

FACTS

Location
The resorts of Davos (5,118 ft) and Klosters (4,000 ft) are just South of the Austrian frontier and North of St Moritz, situated in the Silvretta area of German-speaking Switzerland. Development began at the turn of the century.

Ski areas
Pischa (8,153 ft), Jakobshorn (8,500 ft), Bramabuel (8,126 ft), Riner-horn (8,170 ft) and Schatzalp-Strela (up to 9,262 ft). There is a wide variety of pistes and choice of runs, suitable for skiers of all standards, and also a series of marked runs and cross-country skiing. Klosters has 4 cablecars and several gondolas, ski lifts and chair lifts. The Davos areas has over 30 lifts.

Accommodation
A good range of hotels; the resort is also well provided with restaurants and nightclubs.

Activities
The largest skating rink in Europe plus other rinks, ice hockey, curling, riding, horsedrawn sleighing, tobog-ganing, the largest ski school in Switzerland. Kindergarden in Bramabüel-Jakobshorn.

down Drostobel, although pitched at quite an angle, is so well cambered that it is a pleasure to tackle. Klosters manages to remain a village – though a large and prosperous one. It has always been patronized by so-called 'Beautiful People' and keeps up its reputation today as Prince Charles's favorite ski resort.

Visitors to Davos come from all over the world and from every walk of life, though it has particularly strong links with the medical profession. Like many of Switzerland's resorts, it went through a period when the ailing rich (particularly those suffering from tuberculosis) were sent to benefit from the pure air of the mountains. Many of its hotels started as clinics and there is today one of the world's best hospitals at Davos Platz. Since it has a well-equipped congress centre it often hosts medical conventions. The skier who is accident prone will be comforted to learn that there are many resident doctors as well as dentists, masseurs and a health institute.

The buses which wind along the valley roads give skiers a chance to wander far away from the top lift stations across the Alpine meadows and be brought back from remote villages to the town at no cost. The liftpass acts as a bus ticket too. The roads are kept well cleared and Swiss regularity insures that there are no long cold waits. The buses also supplement the lift capacity of 32,000 skiers an hour though with such a big supply of beds (20,000) it is inevitable that queues tend to build up, particularly for the Parsenn railway. Good skiers buy regional passes and there are cheaper passes for each separate area.

Originally Davos was divided into the little town of Platz and the ski resort of Dorf nearby. Now they have grown together though skiers still tend to live at the Dorf end from which the Parsenn railway rises. The town is very well equipped for the non-skier. The main skating rink is a huge 36,000 square yards of natural ice, the largest in Europe. There are several other rinks, too, and a wide range of activities to sample or watch: ice hockey, curling, riding on horseback or in horsedrawn sleighs, and a challenging toboggan run.

Davos has excellent restaurants ranging from an unexpectedly good and cheap one in Migros Supermarket to the *haute cuisine* of the Landhaus Laret which lies along the road between Davos Dorf and Klosters. The many mountain restaurants on the slopes are big, clean, and warm, with appetizing food. There are many excellent hotels, perhaps with less panache than those of Davos's neighbor to the south, St Moritz, but offering friendly and efficient care for their guests. Despite the ban on discos there are no fewer than 16 nightclubs with live music.

Davos may not be romantic and it is certainly not cheap but it has built up a great reputation of caring for its guests. For a long while tourists have come to enjoy its many ski areas which have been well opened up for them and are kept pisted and patroled. Down in the town the streets bustle with life both by day and by night.

following page
Davos-Klosters map ▶

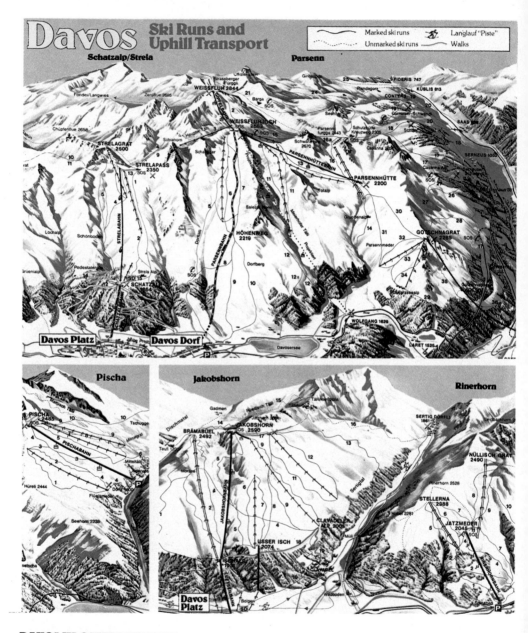

DAVOS KLOSTERS SKI FACTS

Top station 9,300 ft / 2 mountain railways / 6 cable cars /
Many chairs and drags / Maximum rise 3,620 ft /

SWITZERLAND

Zermatt

map *page 32*

Zermatt is a truly great ski resort which, in spite of its size, remains a ski-mountaineering village. No traffic is allowed to disturb the streets, which are lined with deep-eaved wooden chalets. The diversity of its quite difficult slopes lures good skiers from all over the world.

A cemetary may not be a traditional tourist attraction but Zermatt's is well worth visiting, for its old tilting stones and wrought-iron plaques bear the names of many famous climbers who lost their lives in attempts on the great mountain which overshadows the town. The mountaineering museum displays the rope which broke when Edward Whymper's party were descending after their first successful ascent of

Zermatt
*Swiss National
Tourist Office*

the Matterhorn in July, 1865. Half the party were killed in a 4,000 ft fall on that fatal return journey.

Zermatt is still a mountaineering center and its guides take ski mountaineers to conquer for themselves the many peaks which lie within its reach. Monte Rosa, Castor, Pollux, the Breithorn, are all approachable from Zermatt. Then, too, Zermatt is on the classic Haute Route, a high traverse across the crest of the Alps. Skiers make their way from Saas-Fee, adjoining Zermatt, over glaciers and across cols to Verbier further West. They sleep in mountain huts, carrying food, crampons and ice-axes with them and fixing skins to the soles of their skis to trudge upwards. This is high country with all the danger but also all the fascination of altitude.

Winter visitors first came to Zermatt in 1927, following the summer mountaineers, and the railway train up to Riffelberg started a year later. There are easy slopes here, with a superb view of the Monte Rosa. The railway now goes on up to Gornergrat from which a two-stage cableway continues the ascent to Hohtäligrat and Stockhorn (11,170 ft). Competent skiers enjoy the long North-facing runs from here to Gant or Findeln.

A high speed underground train was opened in 1980 up to Sunnegga to help cope with the large crowds that tend to clog the bottom stations in the mornings. From Sunnegga, lifts, gondolas and cables open up the Blauherd-Unter Rothorn slopes. A third area is served by the Schwarzsee lift, which starts at the Winkelmatten end of the village. This network leads on up to the Theodule Pass and Testa Grigia at 11,410 ft. Zermatt has made great efforts to build new lifts. Beds for 16,000 visitors and an uphill transport capacity for 25,000 skiers per hour insure that it is possible to avoid lines during the day, but each morning crowds still jostle impatiently in the pens, waiting for their first lift out of the village.

Although there are nursery areas at Riffelberg and Sunnegga, Zermatt's great appeal is to the intermediate and good skier. From the village at 5,315 ft there are steep wooded slopes up to 7,000 ft and then high rolling uplands right up to a lung-stretching 12,533 ft. With plenty of North-facing slopes, good snow right down to the village insures a normal season from December to May. The lifts on the Theodule glacier and the Klein Matterhorn – the highest aerial cableway in Europe – are open for summer skiing from May to September. Apart from nearly 100 miles of safe, swept pistes, it is the beautiful variety of slopes between which fascinates skiers from all over the world. Endless variations can be searched out in steep gullies or through the forests which clothe the lower slopes.

Always popular is a visit to Cervinia, reached from the Theodule Pass and Testa Grigia on the Italian side of the Matterhorn. The journey down to a bowl of spaghetti and a bottle of Chianti takes medium skiers about an hour and opens up another world. Cervinia was purpose-built for skiers by Mussolini before the Second World War. He destroyed the old village of Breuil, even replacing its French name and calling his smart new resort after the Italian name for the Matterhorn, Cervino.

The village does not have the character of Zermatt. The pistes are

FACTS

Location
Zermatt (4,422 ft) lies in the German-speaking Mattertal valley of Switzerland, in the Alpi Pennine region, in the shadow of the Matterhorn (14,679 ft). Development began in 1927. An enchanting, traffic-free village.

Ski areas
Riffelberg (7,050 ft), Sunegga (6,252 ft), the Theodule glacier and Klein Matterhorn (11,410 ft); and Saas-Fee (nursery to intermediate); Cervinia (in Italy, 6,726 ft). Skiing for all standards. Over 30 lifts in the Zermatt region.

Accommodation
From great hotels to apartment blocs. Plenty of night life.

Activities
Ski mountaineering and touring, bob sleighing, horsedrawn sleighing.

long and comparatively easy, with confidence-inspiring run-outs, but they lack the variety of those on the Swiss side, partly perhaps because Cervinia is built above the treeline at 6,726 ft. But the visit makes a good day's outing from Zermatt and if the return cablecars get stopped by high winds, as they sometimes do, then there is plenty of lively nightlife to sample on the Italian side.

Also on the Italian side is a Flying Kilometer track on which time trials are held regularly to determine the fastest skier and the fastest skis in the world. Ski manufacturers sponsor racers to bring publicity for their products. With grotesque aerodynamic helmets the skiers plummet like torpedoes down the vertiginous drop attaining speeds over 125 mph. An international bobsleigh run provides visitors to Cervinia with the spectacle of another icy chute.

The Mattertal in which Zermatt lies is German-speaking, though Italy is just to the South and the people of the Val d'Herens to the West speak French. Zermatt has its own mini-climate. Often its slopes are well-covered when its neighbors' lack snow; or rocks show through the lower slopes while the resorts surrounding it are snow covered.

Typical of the challenge for holiday skiers at Zermatt is the Luttman-Johnson race, run each year by the Ski Club of Great Britain. Its bizarre rules lay down that as great a mileage as possible must be covered within a set time, while the minutes spent drinking in restaurants count for bonus points. Knowledge of the slopes and the lift system, as well as luck, skiing ability and a strong head for alcohol all play their part in deciding the winner. Only Zermatt provides so many choices of route.

The lazy, too are not forgotten. Zermatt has a heliport from which less energetic skiers can be taken and dropped on nearby mountain slopes for long remote runs.

To the North East of Zermatt, and reached by railway, is Saas-Fee. This is another old village which has banned cars and which is used by ski-mountaineers. There is less intermediate skiing here, though the nursery slopes are good. It is best visited from mid-February onwards, for the high peaks which surround it keep the sun out of the village earlier in the year.

Zermatt's development has been strictly controlled by its tourist director, Constant Cachin, and by the village families of Julens, Perrens and Seilers who have lived there for generations and own most of the land and hotels. It has truly great hotels in the Mont Cervin, the Zermatterhof and the Monte Rosa, which combine superb service with great character. Huge apartment blocks have been built to accommodate the tourists but even they are built in chalet shapes. Very little building land now remains, so each year the prices rise. Nightclubs abound, with The Village in the Hotel de la Poste attracting a big crowd of the young. Lots of bars provide a well-beaten circuit by night.

The railway contributed towards Zermatt's development and visitors must still leave their cars at Täsch, to travel the last few miles by train. Residents can use a big carpark just below the village. But arrival by train has the great charm of being met by horsedriven sleighs waiting to carry passengers and their baggage through the snowy streets to their hotels.

ZERMATT SKI FACTS
Top station 12,491 ft / 2 mountain railways / 8 cable cars /
2 cabins / Many chairs and drags / Maximum rise 3,146 ft /

For the good skier, days pass in Zermatt exploring new ways down
from the many lifts or climbing the surrounding peaks with their
superb slopes. Wandering through the picturesque village in the
early evening is always a delight before settling into a bar or a
discotheque for the night. The high altitude, the sophistication, the
variety of the skiing all put demands on the most energetic skiers and
provide them with an enormously rewarding vacation.

Over the village rears the head of the Matterhorn. Like a prima
donna always displaying her best profile, its sharp pyramid remains
instantly recognizable from any viewpoint. It brought the first visitors
to Zermatt and it watches over the village today like a friendly giant.

SWITZERLAND

Verbier

Verbier is for the adventurous. As one of
Switzerland's few purpose-built-for-skiers resorts, it is surrounded by
magnificent slopes over which the lift system has been gradually
extended until it now joins ten villages. The site chosen thirty years ago
was a mile or two above an old hamlet and not far from the Super Saint

VERBIER SKI FACTS
Top station 9,885 ft / 4 cable cars / 9 cabins / 14 chairs /
34 drags / Maximum rise 2,943 ft (Summer skiing) /

Bernard Hospice on the old route between Italy and Switzerland.

The village of Verbier is set on a wide sunny plateau at 5,000 ft. From the start the planners decreed that buildings should be set parallel to the slopes; that they should have pitched roofs of slate, and walls covered with wood. What they did not expect was that so many chalets would be built until the village spread untidily all over the nearby slopes. After a heavy snowfall, clearing the pathways is a major problem.

Two main lift systems start from Verbier. Savolèyres has South-facing slopes back to Verbier and over the other side to Tzoumaz. This is the place for bad weather, when the scattered trees help visibility. The second system starts with a gondola from Medran up to Ruinettes where there is an open sunny bowl at Lac des Vaux for medium skiers. From Ruinettes the two-stage Attelas cablecar rises to Mont Gelé (9,842 ft). Here, and at Tortin past Lac des Vaux, the bump bombers will find steep, sometimes icy slopes.

These village lifts are gateways to a huge area stretching from Les Collons in the East to Le Châble in the West, linking the four valleys of Val de Bagnes, Val de Nendaz, Val d'Heremance and Mayen de Riddes. Eighty lifts can carry 30,000 skiers an hour and cover 180 miles of marked runs including a pisted circuit of the four valleys. Those who do not want to stay in Verbier can choose instead the new village of Super Nendaz, or the big rather ugly modern complex of Thyon 2000. Some of the old villages remain, like Mayens de Sion below the beautiful piste de l'Ours. There is always a lift to link into the main network.

But the young, energetic skiers who go to Verbier look for more than pistes and this is superb touring country. Verbier is set at one end of the Haute Route which starts at Saas Fee, so there are great ski tours to the Rosablanche and other peaks. Even the intermediate skier will enjoy the long sunny run down from the Super St Bernard to Italy. The little area of Champex-Lac makes an interesting excursion. Ten minutes contouring a slope from the top of a lift opens up hidden valleys. After every snowfall there are dozens of unmarked, unserviced slopes to be explored afresh.

The Ecole de Ski Fantastique gives courses in deep snow or on spring snow. It organizes pre-season get-fit courses, gives lessons on how to cope with steep couloirs and guides parties on ski safaris to visit small villages. More ambitious (and well-heeled) skiers can go by helicopter to far-away glaciers; more energetic ones can climb there on their skins.

Every year sees the opening of new lifts. Behind Mont Gelé lies the Mont Fort at 10,919 ft. With a steep face at the top, it gives long, even downhill runs across a glacier and then tips down to join the existing Mont-Gelé-Tortin run. This is high country and glaciers mean crevasses, so care must be taken.

Verbier is made for expeditions. Every morning brings a new test of skill or bravery: the circuit of the four valleys, a tour with a mountain peak to scale, or simply a pleasant day's ski to a favorite restaurant. There are several good eating places on the slopes: chez Philippe's and La Fougère at Tzoumaz, and Monsieur Buison's at Le Châble tempt skiers to while away the afternoon. One of the Haute Route touring huts, the Mont Fort (to the West of the Mont Fort lift) has been caught up in the new lift system and so has adapted itself to serve ham, cheese and soup for lunch to skiers willing to go just off the beaten track.

All nationalities come to Verbier and many of the international set at Geneva have chalets there. There are some good hotels but most of the young who flock to Verbier prefer to stay in chalets and this gives a lively, informal atmosphere to the night life. It is chalet-visiting rather than nightclubs which keeps the midnight oil burning. There are good bars to start the evening. At Le Pub serried rows of drinkers stand seven or eight deep round the bar. The Farm gets crowded, too, later on but with the dancing separate from a large bar and sitting area, it is not so dark and squashed.

One of the specialities of the Valais Canton in which Verbier lies is *raclette*. A huge disc of Swiss cheese is held close to a flaming wood fire until it melts. As the cheese begins to flow it is poured over jacket potatoes. Dôle de Sion, the good red wine pressed from grapes grown in the valley below, accompanies *raclette* perfectly.

Verbier offers skiing for the adventurous, the young and the energetic. It also has areas for those who want smooth, gentle slopes to flatter their lack of technique. In the mountain restaurant of Ruinettes where skiers come off the steep slopes of Mont Gelé and Tortin as well as the gentle Lac des Vaux area, the racing pants of the experts mingle with the salopettes of the two-week-a-year holiday skiers. The slopes are well planned and the off-piste skiing is inexhaustible.

Location
Purpose-built Verbier (5,000 ft) in French-speaking Switzerland, was constructed for skiers in the 1950s on the Swiss side of Martigny, set where the Rhône does a great right angle turn from the West toward Geneva 75 miles to the North. The region is also known as the Four Valleys.

Ski areas
Les Collons to Le Châble, the Haute Route region, Champex-Lac, Mont Gelé-Tortin. Verbier offers skiing for the adventurous, the young and the energetic. There are over 60 ski lifts.

Accommodation
Chalets predominate amongst the hotels, both in Verbier, and Super Nendaz and Thyon; restaurants are scattered throughout the ski areas; good night life.

Activities
Touring; there is also a ski school and heliskiing.

SWITZERLAND
St Moritz

*S*t Moritz has for so long been connected with wealth and aristocracy that the very name evokes princes and casinos, furcoats and horsedrawn sleighs as well as ski slopes. It is true that only half its visitors go to St Moritz to ski, yet it is surrounded by slopes of infinite variety, networked by more than forty lifts. Expensively dressed crowds visit the resort to watch horses racing across the frozen lake; international sportsmen test their courage down the Cresta Run; playboys chance their money at the Casino and the wealthy trim their figures at health clinics. For the skier all this is just the background to a great vacation spent crisscrossing the 250 miles of pistes, exploring the slopes of the Engadine mountains or jogging along the crosscountry paths.

Horse-riding in snow at St Moritz (Giegel)
Swiss National Tourist Office

The town itself is divided into the older Dorf to the North and the more recently developed Bad to the South. St Moritz Dorf is where the great hotels such as the Kulm, the Carlton and the turreted Palace lie, surrounded by expensive boutiques. The narrow crowded streets wind steeply up from the lake. St Moritz Bad, along the valley floor, contains

ST MORITZ SKI FACTS
Top station 10,801 ft / 2 mountain railways / 5 cable cars /
1 cabin / 1 chair / 50 drags / Maximum rise 3,842 ft /

dozens of cheaper hotels and restaurants, supermarkets and ski hire shops and, as its name implies, a superb swimming pool with natural spring water.

From Dorf, the Corviglia railway climbs to 8,000 ft and brings the skier to the center of a network of three cablecars and sixteen lifts, one of which rises to Piz Nair at 10,000 ft. The Signalbahn cablecar comes up from St Moritz Bad so that both parts of the resort are linked to this main area. The slopes, mainly South and East facing, are suitable for every standard of skier. The 40 piste beating machines owned by St Moritz keep the whole mountainside prepared and the 400 instructors work here with their ski school classes. One of the great moments after a day spent skiing above the treeline comes on the way down towards the halfway station at Chantarella, when the tang of pines and woodsmoke rises from the forest, and the town can be seen below, laid out along the shore of the lake.

It is in the Corviglia ski area that the International Ski Federation has authorized race courses, for St Moritz has a long tradition of ski racing. The area is on the World Cup circuit and the Winter Olympics have been held there twice. The ski school organizes its own races on quite another scale. Anyone can take part, whether they are able to clip accurately through a maze of gates or just stagger from one slalom pole to another.

But there is far more skiing round St Moritz than lies above the town itself. A Sportbus (included on the liftpass) runs regularly between Lagalb, ten miles to the South East, via St Moritz to Sils, six miles to the South West. With its help the skier can use the many cablecars along the route and explore the areas they serve.

Over Christmas and the New Year, as well as in the mid-February to March period when fashionable people like to be seen in St Moritz, Range-Rovers and the new 4-wheel drive Subarus clutter the car parks at the cablecar stations and there can be long delays. At these times the ticket offices issue reservations so that those who wait can at least do so at a nearby café rather than stand queueing uncomfortably in their ski boots. Because fashion is important in St Moritz, these problems tend to disappear during the low January period.

A few minutes by Sportbus from St Moritz Bad is Surlej village where the Corvatsch cablecar rises to 11,320 ft. Here in winter, there are several long and satisfying runs for the good skier both on piste and off. Since the area faces North, the snow stays in good condition, though it can be cold early in the year. Later, because of the situation and height, there is sufficient snow cover for both lifts and ski school to continue working into the summer.

Further along the valley towards the Maloja Pass is the village of Sils Maria, from which another cablecar and six lifts open up the easy slopes of Furtschellas.

Lagalb, near the Bernina Pass, offers more difficult skiing from 9,500 ft down mile-and-a-half runs which include steep mogul slopes. These can be testing, even for the expert skier. The Diavolezza area lies above Pontresina where the old houses are painted with murals of country life. The slopes are easy and the main piste cuts a broad swaithe down the mountainside. Here, too, is one of the classic runs of

FACTS

Location
St Moritz lies by its lake in the Bernina region of the predominantly German-speaking region of Switzerland.

Ski areas
Piz Nair (10,000 ft), Lagalb (9,500 ft), Corviglia, Corvatsch, Furtschellas, Diavolezza, the Morteratsch glacier. There are 75 miles of cross-country tracks, 60 lifts and skiing of every standard.

Accommodation
Runs the gamut from the great palace hotels to cheaper accommodation; night life ranges from the expensive and sophisticated to the cheaper discos.

Activities
Hang gliding, bob sleighing and tobogganing, horse racing on ice, curling and golf on ice, swimming pool with natural spring water, ski school, touring and tracked cross-country skiing.

the Alps, the Morteratsch Glacier, down five miles amidst spectacular scenery. A guide is needed to prevent falls into a crevasse.

Even the best skier could spend two weeks exploring the pistes of Corviglia, Corvatsch, Furtschellas, Diavolezza and Lagalb, yet there are many more beaten areas within easy reach of the center of St Moritz. Lying between them and stretching out on every side are slopes which give first rate opportunities for easy touring. From the tops of the cablecars the good skier needs only a guide and the energy to walk for a few minutes to get far from the crowds and onto untracked snow, with the peaks of the Engadine forming a sensational background.

For crosscountry skiing, St Moritz is one of the best-prepared resorts in Switzerland. There are 75 miles of track round the lake and through the woods, and the skischool is just as well-qualified to teach Nordic as Alpine skiing. The greatest crosscountry ski race in the world – the Engadine Ski Marathon – takes place from Maloja to Zuoz each March, passing St Moritz. More than 12,000 competitors, of all ages and standards, jostle along the 25 miles. It is an exhausting race for the amateur crosscountry skier and a kaleidoscopic spectacle for the crowds who watch.

There is so much to do in St Moritz apart from skiing that it is no wonder that many who go never put on skis. This is the playground of royalty, film stars and Eurocrats. From Hanselman's – the place for tea – the cosmopolitan crowd pour into the main street, always well-, sometimes exotically dressed; even the children wear fur coats! The rich have their own chalets or stay in the great hotels, of which the Palace is the greatest. The Badrutt family, which runs the Palace, started the whole idea of winter sports when in 1864 they invited a party of English to see that Switzerland was sunny even in winter. They won their bet and winter visitors have been coming ever since.

Nightlife at St Moritz can be the ultimate in sophistication. The Suvretta House, set in its own grounds high above St Moritz Bad, has a French restaurant, Le Miroir, and dancing to an Argentinian orchestra in its La Volière bar. Evening dress is indispensable. Kings Club, in the Palace Hotel, also caters for the rich or aristocratic. But in contrast just up the road is the Pianoroom, where a bottle of ordinary wine can be enjoyed to the accompaniment of jazz on the piano, at very reasonable cost. The Chesa Veglia offers an atmosphere of antiquity while Steffanis has a formal bar upstairs and a more lively one, Le Malibu, below. There are dozens of discotheques to suit any taste and pocket.

Every conceivable winter sport is practised in St Moritz, including the very newest such as hang-gliding. The bobsleigh and toboggan runs are the only ones made of natural ice in the Alps. To watch the four-man bobs thundering down the icy chute and swinging up on the corners to scrabble high up along the walls, is to witness one of the most breathtaking sights in sports. From the bridges over the Cresta Run drivers can be seen steering with the most sensitive shifts of weight as they hurtle down.

The great lake beside the Palace Hotel is as much a part of the life of the resort as the mountains which surround it. The ice freezes thick and firm, making an excellent surface for the horse races which are held

there regularly. Tourists can try ski-joring, which involves being towed over the ice on skis behind a horse! Recently the town has started hosting winter golf tournaments on the ice and curling competitions involving as many as a hundred teams sliding their flat stones across the smooth surface.

St Moritz is a great resort for a group which includes non-skiers as well as skiers. The richness of its facilities draws sportsmen from all over the world to experience the thrills of speed and hazard. No-one could be bored with so much to see and to try. In addition the skier has open to him the immense variety of the Engadine Mountains, which are linked to St Moritz by fast and reliable transport.

The Cresta Run at St Moritz (*Giegel*)
Swiss National Tourist Office

FRANCE

The Three Valleys

Val d'Isère
Tignes

La Plagne
Les Arcs

FRANCE

The Three Valleys

maps
pages 44–45

Courchevel   Meribel
Menuires   Val Thorens

The catchphrase of the French valleys of St Bon, Les Allues and Les Belleville is 'the greatest skiable region in the world' and 250 miles of marked runs served by around 150 lifts make this a difficult boast to beat.

Future developments are unlikely to upset the claim, for other vast areas such as Val d'Isère, Les Arcs and La Plagne are more likely than not to link up with the Three Valleys as they expand. Already the other regions are within reach of the Three Valleys by a competent offpiste skier, though at present a guide is needed and the journey may involve a night stop in a mountain hut.

Of the four major resorts in the Three Valleys each has its own claim. Fashionable Courchevel offers skiing for pleasure; Meribel considers itself to be the heart of the region; Menuires claims it provides skiing without restriction and Val Thorens that it has perfect snow in all four seasons.

Courchevel is certainly a resort of superlatives. Biggest and most westerly of the stations, it consists of three villages known by their heights in metres above sea level as: 1,550, 1,650 and 1,850. Together they have 27,000 beds, 62 lifts carrying 45,000 skiers an hour (insuring no queues) and 100 miles of downhill skiing. Crosscountry skiing, hang gliding and parachuting can all be learnt there. Wealthy visitors fly into the altiport by air taxi or private plane.

Everything is done to pamper the skier at Courchevel. At dawn an army of piste machines chunter out to groom the slopes of the main areas of La Loze, Saulire, Biolley and Moriond. Some of the wide boulevards are so gentle that the most geriatric of skiers can slide slowly down, enjoying the sunshine and the mountain views without fear of falling. Yet there is sufficient scope for very energetic recreational skiers to explore new areas each day and experts will find steep downhills like the Jean Blanc run to challenge their skill. Each summer, runs are regrassed and the rocks which have emerged are removed. Then as soon as a few inches of snow have fallen there is a smooth safe surface over which to ski.

There are three ski schools (one in each village) which teach both downhill and crosscountry skiing. The schools also provide guides to lead small parties of good skiers away from the pistes over the untracked slopes which extend in every direction.

There are no fewer than 22 sports shops, 16 boutiques, 8 hairdressers and 5 jewelry stores to tempt Courchevel's rich visitors in the three villages, plus skating rinks, heated swimming pools and solariums; there are also 62 hotels, 44 restaurants (11 of them on the slopes) and 7 nightclubs. Yet Courchevel is always full. It does not require publicity, and tour operators search in vain for free beds. Recently a central station has been built to house gondolas, tourist office, ski hire shops and restaurants, but most of the buildings sprawl around the mountain side. The resort is not cheap but it is very, very well equipped.

Even culture is not forgotten. An international cultural exchange center (known by its French initials as FACIM) is housed in a beautiful piece of architecture on the slopes beside Courchevel 1,850. Jazz, film and music festivals are held, as well as conferences, and there is a language laboratory to which the local ski instructors were sent when it opened.

Courchevel and Meribel in the next valley, are perfect examples of what the French call their 'second generation' resorts. A first generation resort is one developed from an existing village. It often has old buildings and a picturesque church. Most are built on old mountain passes and roads, cluttered with cars which run through the middle. Skilifts are set up one by one by local farmers for their own convenience rather than that of skiers. Builders are allowed to put chalets on the ski slopes. Planning is by local parish councils, which are sometimes overwhelmed by the sudden influx of tourists and anxious to preserve their grazing rights.

Second generation resorts are built on previously empty sites in the mountains. A whole area is acquired by a syndicate, often with the help of government money. Roads, electricity and water are installed and the development of village and lift system is planned carefully. It is usually possible to ski back to a hotel or chalet in a second generation resort, though cars clutter the streets and roads have to be cleared and gritted.

Like many second generation resorts, Courchevel put up its first lifts in 1947. Meribel, in the next valley, was just a year ahead and it had been planned even before the war. When Germany annexed Austria a British colonel, Peter Lindsay, decided to leave the Arlberg and Salzburgerland and look instead for a ski region in France. He found the long North South valley of Les Allues up from Brides-les-Bains to Les Allues, characterized by rolling Alps unlikely to avalanche and open sunny slopes. With a syndicate of friends, he had a road constructed in 1938 and the first buildings went up in 1939. After the war he came back and the first lift, Burgin, was constructed on the eastern side. By 1950 the connexion was made with Courchevel.

The syndicate had strong ideas about development and insisted that all the buildings should be stone, woodclad chalets with slate roofs

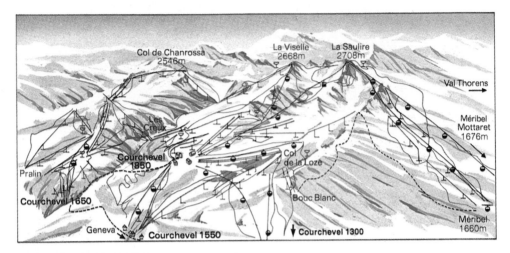

COURCHEVEL SKI FACTS
Top station 8,855 ft / Over 40 lifts including 10 cabins. Connects with
Meribel and Val Thorens for another 100 lifts. / Maximum rise 3,375 ft /

made of local ardois. The Arolla pines and the Savoyard atmosphere
were preserved. Even today a small group of the original forty or so
chalets are lived in by top people while colorful shops, and typical
Savoyard cafés and crêperies wind down the long main street to the
tourist office which is the present center.

Because Meribel remained comparatively small and undiscovered
until the early seventies, it became popular with those avoiding
publicity. Brigitte Bardot, for example, came to enjoy her vacations
away from newspapermen. The original club atmosphere kept the
village discreet, none felt the need to display riches.

But in 1972 Meribel had to take a big decision. Should it expand to
keep pace with the enormous development taking place in the
adjoining valleys, and could it do so without changing its character? It
was decided to expand and the planning was done so well that the style
of Meribel itself has not changed; 65% of Meribel's guests are still
regulars.

First some big apartments were built, still in Savoyard style, on the
edge of the village. Then, in 1975, Meribel Mottaret was opened. This
satellite, a couple of miles from the main village, is at 5,412 ft and the
height insures snow even if Meribel itself (at a few hundred feet lower)
is a little bare. It provides what can be described as a bypass on the
main route between Courchevel and Menuires in the third valley, yet
runs and lifts connect with those of the main village. The architecture of
Meribel Mottaret still follows the Savoyard style but on a large scale,
with apartments, shops and restaurants built within vast wood faced
chalets.

The two Meribels have expanded to offer 17,000 beds yet cunningly
without creating a big town impression. The small woods that stud the

area, giving character to the slopes and crosscountry trails also giving a rustic atmosphere to the chalets.

Like Courchevel, Meribel caters well for its clients. The altiport has regular connections with the Geneva and Lyons-Satolas airports. Among the well-laid out pistes is a steep one down which competitions are held. Attractive crosscountry trails are laid out through the little woods. It is even possible to learn how to control a car on ice in a special driving school run by rally drivers.

If Courchevel and Meribel are second generation resorts, where development is planned ahead with the skier in mind, then Menuires in the Valley of Belleville is an excellent example of the 'third generation'. According to this pattern, all the facilities are housed in one building. In Menuires it forms a horseshoe, with covered corridors linking apartments, restaurants, and shops.

When, as happens at 6,070 ft, great storms deposit several feet of snow overnight no one is woken by the angry snarl of snow ploughs clearing the streets. Within the complex all streets are covered. Cars and buses are allowed to special access points outside the horseshoe to deposit baggage and then kept in special parks. From inside the horseshoe the skier has only to walk across the snow to the lifts which rise from it. Some buildings give direct access to lifts. At night there is no need to put on an overcoat to visit a restaurant; by day people who are cooking in their own apartment stay within the main complex when buying food at the supermarket. The lack of outside walls makes the buildings cheaper to heat, while outside the altitude insures good snow conditions.

The Menuires slopes are generally above the treeline. As in the other Three Valley resorts, the pistes are well groomed and cleared of rocks. There are 80 instructors in the ski school, though not many speak English. Young in its appeal, Menuires makes a feature of freestyle. It

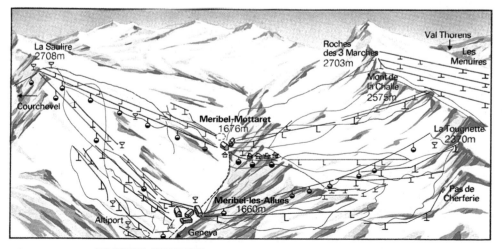

MERIBEL SKI FACTS
Top station 8,839 ft / Over 40 lifts including 7 cabins. Connects with Courchevel and Val Thorens for another 100 lifts. / Maximum rise 3,379 ft /

can be learnt by holiday skiers or they may prefer to watch the thrilling display during the international competitions when experts somersault into the air. Free style competitions have three elements: aerials, where competitors leap, twisting and somersaulting, off a specially constructed jump; moguls, where they hurtle down a bump slope, jumping or rolling as they speed down; and ballet where they dance, turn and ski gracefully down smooth gentle slopes.

Après ski, as suits a young resort, is unsophisticated. Five discos, a cinema and a bowling alley make sure there is sufficient variety for the evening and there are good restaurants. A heated outdoor pool is popular in the evenings.

Val Thorens, at 7,546 ft with lifts up to 11,250 ft, lies up the valley of Belleville from Menuires. Outwardly unattractive, its site can be windy and bleak but the snow is superb. It opened in 1973 after fighting for years against conservationists who delayed the building of an essential cablecar in the Park National de la Vanoise. Five glaciers, including Polcet, Thorens and Chavière come within its lift network, offering perfect late-season skiing. There are many easy blue runs and several steep slopes. The round trip to Courchevel and back covers 50 miles of varied skiing.

The buildings, which include five hotels with beds for 5,000, look austere and the après ski is not important. This is a resort for serious skiers and it concentrates on the sport.

The Three Valleys offer a great ski vacation for those who have, and demand, everything. The glaciers above Val Thorens keep their snow and extend its season even when the sun burns day after day from a dark blue sky. All four resorts offer an unrivaled ski area which is beautifully prepared. Courchevel and Meribel in particular are not cheap but they cater for connoisseurs with expensive tastes.

FACTS

Location	Resorts	Accommodation	Activities
The three valleys of St Bon, Les Allues and Les Belleville in the great French Alpine ski area which includes Val d'Isère and Tignes, Les Arcs and La Plagne; the Italian frontier is to the East, Geneva and Lausanne to the North.	Courchevel and Meribel (2nd generation resorts developed from the 1940s onwards), Menuires (3rd generation, opened in 1973) and Val Thorens. Courchevel (62 lifts) and Meribel (40 lifts) offer skiing for all standards over 250 miles of marked runs. Menuires and especially Val Thorens are for serious skiers.	Several thousands of beds throughout the four resorts; the night life ranges from sophisticated in Courchevel to almost none in Val Thorens.	Crosscountry skiing, hang gliding, parachuting, several schools, extensive shopping in Courchevel, heated pools and solariums, skating; jazz, film and music festivals.

Val d'Isère
Tignes

map *page 48*

There is nothing cosy or picturesque about Val d'Isère. It is an efficient *station de ski* built with a good deal of outside influence. Much of the direction and the money for development has come from Paris. Some of its promoters come from Italy, for it is within a few miles of the Italian border though all the routes are closed in winter. More unexpected is the influence of Alsace. Several families emigrated from this area on the far side of France during the early part of the century. The families of the Val d'Isère champions Jean-Claude Killy and the Goitschel sisters, each of whom won medals in the 1964 and 1968 Olympics, all originated in Alsace.

Foreign influence is all pervasive. Every enthusiastic ski bum in the world wants to come to this great ski center to work or ski through a season.

The heart of Val d'Isère is a large arcaded semi circle of shops and hotels. What makes the heart beat is a modern three-storey tourist office with accommodation bureau, lift ticket office, Club des Sports and a radio station.

In contrast, tucked away behind a big Club Mediterranée hotel on the opposite corner of the street is what remains of the old quarter. The church goes back to 1533. This was originally where the Dukes of Savoy had their hunting lodge on an old pass to Lanslebourg and the Mont Cenis. Little is made of the old quarter today. It is surrounded by roads and hotels. The ski school opened in 1934. The lift Solaise went up in 1943 and the resort is now developing so fast that seven or eight new lifts are opened each season.

What is important at Val d'Isère is not the village but the skiing. Two cablecars rise from the village itself, up the South West facing Solaise and the North East facing Bellevarde. A gondola from La Daille, a couple of miles North West down the road towards Bourg St Maurice and the valley, climbs in two sections to meet the top of the Bellevarde lift at 12,106 ft. In 1972 another cablecar was built a few miles higher up towards the Col de l'Iseran at Le Fornet and this links into the network

served by the Solaise lift. A bus shuttles frequently and regularly
between the four lift stations, distributing clattering groups of skiers
and skis so that lines do not build up at any of the valley stations.
Above, 57 lifts cast a web over the slopes.

The runs through the woods to the lower stations are fairly steep and
some of them, such as the East face of Bellevarde, are classic black
runs. But once above the treeline the slopes are more gentle and up
here the medium skier finds mile upon mile of well networked slopes.
On a clear day it is possible to look across from the top of one lift to the
top of another on a nearby ridge. After a long ski down, then the lift up,
there is another panorama with more lifts and runs to explore. The
seemingly endless succession, together with a virtual absence of
queues, beguiles the medium skier into covering enormous mileages.

Every possible orientation means that a thoughtful, knowledgeable
skier can always find powder or spring snow right through to the
summer season. Within a radius of 6 miles there are 35 peaks and cols
between 9,800 and 12,000 ft. It is possible to sit at the top of Bellevarde
with a wonderful panorama of Mont Blanc, the Sana, Grande Motte and
Grand Casse ahead and see the international crowds of skiers. The
standard is tremendously high; the clothes are extremely smart.

There is nursery skiing close to the village on the lower slope of
Solaise but really Val d'Isère is wasted on a beginner. Far better to
wait until its variety and scope can be appreciated.

All around the pisted area is great ski touring. The ski school
provides guides for day tours or longer. With its steep drops Val's
slopes can be dangerous if warning notices are ignored. A great deal
of work has been done to prevent avalanches. High up in the gullies,
where the first trickles of snow might gather into an avalanche, concrete
and cast iron barriers have been erected to stabilize them. Great roads

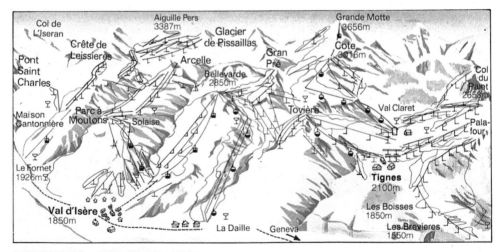

VAL D'ISERE / TIGNES SKI FACTS
Top station 11,955 ft / 4 cable cars / 4 cabins /
Many chairs and drags / Maximum rise 3,066 ft /

have been driven round the contours up on the slopes to catch the snow in large trenches as it starts to move. Nets and fences on steep slopes break up the slides.

Val's army of *pisteurs* is one of the best in the world. Tough and hard working, they bring down potential avalanches with grenades and drive their snowcats through the night flattening the pistes and preparing race courses.

This is one of the premier racing centers of the world. Down from Bellevarde to La Daille runs the OK downhill course, named after two of Val's racing sons, Henri Oreiller and Jean-Claude Killy. As soon as snow starts to fall in October it is beaten into place and throughout the winter season the course is kept for racers, fenced and flagged down the entire length on race days.

The international racing circuit starts each season with the Criterium de la Première Neige at Val d'Isère. As well as being the first event in the World Cup calendar it is also one of the few at which both men and women have downhill and slalom races. There are not many venues where there is sufficient accommodation for the whole circus of racers, officials and servicemen and fewer still which could produce the courses for all the events. It is a witness to the snow sureness of Val d'Isère that this major event can confidently be scheduled to take place as early as the first week in December.

After the Criterium, the course is used for all sorts of races. Paris taxi drivers come one weekend; the Marseilles police another. The first half of January is reserved for the national championships of the Belgians, Danes, Dutch and often the British too. In the Lowlander championships all four nations come together in friendly rivalry. Later in the season even more 'amateur' races take place between the parliamentarians from Britain, Switzerland and France.

Only a resort with the enormous skiable area of Val d'Isère could afford to set aside such an acreage for racers. The timing, provision of results and often the organization are also set up by the resort.

A cluster of buildings, including some huge new apartment blocks, encircle the new Maison de Val d'Isère. There is a wide main street of smart and expensive shops lying on one side of the fast-flowing Isère, and big hotels on the opposite side. Shops, hotels and garages straggle along the roads to Fornet, Solaise and La Daille.

Every kind of accommodation is available, from the humble youth hostel to the luxurious hotel. One of the old hotels, the Christiana, lies back from the main road with the thick old exterior walls and the interior of a small and comfortable chateau. The food, as everywhere in Val d'Isère except the mountain restaurants, is delicious.

The simplest specialities of the region make excellent picnic food. Red Gamay wine or white Apremont washes down a Savoie Tomme cheese. A local beverage to be drunk with care is Groll. It is a mixture of coffee, fresh orange and lemon with Marc spirits served hot in a closed earthenware pot supplied with a separate spout for each person to drink from. It is far too easy to get bewitched into drinking too much through the little spouts.

Night life is not a great feature of a visit to Val d'Isère – the town seems to accept that exhaustion is the general mood after a day on the slopes. For those who want them there are night clubs and a mass of small bars and *crêperies*. Delicious pancakes filled with cheese and ham or soaked in Grand Marnier help to fill the gap between the end of skiing and the start of dinner. There are all sorts of shops too but prices are generally high in this cosmopolitan resort.

Val d'Isère has all the usual facilities such as outdoor rink and swimming pool. A crosscountry course wanders along from Val d'Isère towards La Daille and another is tucked high in the mountains above Solaise round the Ouillette lake.

Val d'Isère is also a summer resort, primarily for the French, with a season which runs from mid-June to mid-August. The lifts work up on the Col de l'Isèran and there is a good non-skiing program of horse riding, swimming, photographic safaris in the Vanoise national park, walks, tennis and so on.

When the French electricity authorities decided to build a huge dam at Tignes they were faced with having to drown the old village. This they eventually did in 1952, after moving the inhabitants to a bowl

FACTS

Location
Skirting the Parco di Gran Paradiso on the Italian side of the frontier, Val d'Isère and Tignes by its lake are in the French Alps South of Geneva and Lausanne. Val d'Isère was begun in the '30s and is still developing; Tignes is a third generation resort of the '50s and expanding fast.

Ski areas
Bellevarde and Solaise, Tovière, Grande Motte (8,178 ft). An area famous for black runs with many facilities for an intermediate skier. The area is served by nearly 60 lifts, including 4 cables, 3 gondolas and 7 chair lifts.

Accommodation
Apartment blocs in both resorts, especially Tignes, which has 20,000 beds; Val d'Isère has great hotels, new hotels, apartments and youth hostels.

Activities
Apart from serious skiing and racing, there is ski touring and crosscountry skiing. Both resorts have summer skiing.

above the treeline at 6,980 ft called Lac de Tignes. The new village had all the potential of a ski resort. Lifts were built up the southern side at Chardonnet, while a chair up the steep Tovière side linked the Val d'Isère's Bellevarde and La Daille areas.

By 1960 there were still only 200 tourist beds but since then mushrooming is the only word to describe Tigne's growth. Today there are more than 20,000 beds in several interlinked *stations*. Val Claret, an agglomeration as big as Lac de Tignes, nestles under the Grande Motte. Le Levachet is linked to Val Claret by a short gondola. Le Rosset is at the bottom of the Tovière lift. Tignes is a third generation resort gone mad with all the villages collected into a bowl, loosely connected and surrounded by lifts.

Finding the best way round is quite difficult for the newcomer but the recreational skier soon finds the lift which will lead back to any particular part of the village. Those staying at Val Claret take the Ballin poma to return to their own front door. Those in Lac de Tignes take Tufs up to Tovière.

The Grande Motte gondola takes skiers up to 11,480 ft and gives access to the whole network of 100 miles of swept runs covered by 57 lifts with 1,500 metres of downhill running. So far lifts have outstripped beds, so that lines are minimal except at high points in French holidays.

There are 35 hotels, many club hotels, chalets and studios but most of the accommodation is in big apartment blocks, formidable to look at but providing super comfort and convenience for the skier. There are dozens of restaurants at which to dine. Fourteen discos show that this is a young people's resort.

Tignes shares Val d'Isère's wide-ranging medium slopes but its black runs are also famous. The moguls down Tovière are said to be the most difficult in Europe. The Double M on the Grande Motte is challenging and le Vallon de la Sache has a stomach-turning vertical drop.

Tignes sporting club organizes regional, national and international Alpine, crosscountry and free style events. Free stylers in particular enjoy the steep slopes for their mogul events, and smooth gentle ones for ballet. Every evening a guide is available to give advice to tourers on conditions in the surrounding mountains. Those willing to walk a bit on their skis can find their way or be guided to La Plagne or Les Arcs.

'Ski 365 days in the year' is no idle boast yet on summer mornings many international Alpine race teams train on the Grande Motte. After lunch they come down to spend the afternoon swimming, playing tennis or walking.

Occasionally, as can happen with near neighbors, Val d'Isère and Tignes fall out over their joint liftpass and visitors are confined to one village area or the other. It is a pity for this is a superb ski region which cannot be separated into two parcels. Powder hounds will find the offpiste a delight, while those whose two weeks skiing a year never quite allow them to become expert or fit, still have the opportunity to roam over a wide-ranging area with ever-changing views.

FRANCE

La Plagne Les Arcs

The French believe that vacations are a time for relaxation. Skiing must be fun. There is already a challenge in the weather, the steepness of the slopes; the physical outdoor effort required from people many of whom spend the rest of their lives working indoor at desks. So the planners of ski resorts must make resorts oases of warmth and color to counteract the awesome effect of the barren wilderness in which they are set.

This is the concept of the third generation resort. The effort of walking to and from the slopes carrying equipment is eliminated. Skiers put on their skis at the door of their hotel or apartment.

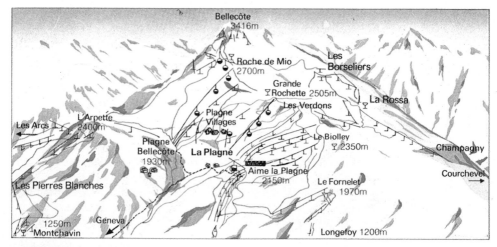

LA PLAGNE SKI FACTS
Top station 11,170 / 1 cable car / 3 cabins /
Many chairs and drags / Maximum rise 2,518 ft /

LES ARCS SKI FACTS
Top station 8,191 ft / 1 cable car /
15 chairs and 35 drags / Maximum rise 2,394 ft /

Restaurants, cinemas and discos are within reach of living quarters
without braving the night air. Although there is plenty of steep terrain
for the good skier to explore, the whole area is also networked with
broad, gentle boulevards to give confidence to the beginner, the
scared or the elderly.

At a time when Austrian and Swiss resorts had stern notices
forbidding skiers to put their skis on inside the top stations of cablecars
(because they caused obstruction), the French at Flaine had built a
large mat-floored room inside the top station so that skiers could be
encouraged to fix their boots into bindings there; to wait for the slowest
members of the group to sort themselves out within shelter, and then
set off together to meet a blizzard in the white desert outside. This kind
of detailed attention to comfort meant that all a skier's efforts and
energies could go into conquering the steep slopes, the most exciting
way down the mountain.

The two regions which have expanded the concept of the third
generation resort to its widest extent are those which lie close to one
another in the Haute Savoie region of France: La Plagne and Les Arcs.

The La Plagne region now includes no less than five high mountain
resorts and three villages down in the valley. From 8 am to 1 pm the

high resorts are connected by cablecar, telebus or shuttlebus. All through the day all eight are joined by skilift and piste. Each complex contains about 6,000 beds, sufficient to make a self-contained unit without sprawling. Each has its own character.

La Plagne itself, the original village, is a rather untidy collection of tower blocks and flat-roofed arcades, like a giant supermarket with accommodation and entertainment packaged into it. Perhaps its most surprising feature is a small Spitfire on a plinth which stands on the site where the RAF dropped supplies to the freedom-fighting maquis during the Second World War. In this great holiday-oriented complex the memory of the days when there was nothing here but a life and death struggle between fighting men, is curiously moving.

Set only half a mile above the mother village, is Plagne Villages. Described by its builders as 'neo-rustic', it consists of two, three and four-storey houses jumbled in picturesque intimacy round a covered marketplace. All the buildings are faced in wood to soften the harshness of its mountain setting.

In contrast, about the same distance in the opposite direction from the mother village lies Aime-La-Plagne, a great three-pointed pyramid of a block built like a steamboat to be buffeted but never rocked by the tempests which surround it. Aime-La-Plagne defies the elements.

Bellecote, at the foot of the glacier slopes, is a long, ten-storey building which follows the contour of the mountain like a giant wave. The last-built mountain village, Belle Plagne, lies on the slopes above Bellecote, again a massive building but clad in wood. Within these last two villages are innumerable apartments, cinemas, swimming pools, discotheques, restaurants and shopping centers.

Below in the valley lie three more villages: the really ancient Champagny, the restored Montchavin which looks more like an Italian seaside resort with its steep-sided circle of buildings; and Montalbert, half old, half new. These were old villages which were in danger of disintegration; their young people leaving for jobs in the industrial towns and their schools closing. Then the wave of tourism swept over them. Finance from Paris built apartment blocks, restaurants and smart hotels. The young people returned to take up jobs on the slopes and in the hotels; schools re-opened and life returned.

Each village has its own character and suits different people. La Plagne itself is very central, like a sun with pistes that ray out to its satellites; Plagne Villages with its central square is convenient for families with small children; teenagers love Aime with its corridors of slot machines – and a language laboratory redresses the cultural balance. Bellecote and Belle Plagne are miracles of packaging and convenience for those who want their own apartments. The valley villages are rural, set down among apple trees and filled with birds. They have the disadvantage that it can take some time on the lifts to reach good snow but they offer cheaper rates than the mountain stations and, unless snow is very scarce, it is possible to ski right back down to them.

All around these village islands lie the immense mountains, crossed by 80 lifts and with 100 miles of beaten piste ranging between 3,800 and 10,000 ft. A sixth of the runs in the La Plagne area are registered as

FACTS

Location
Just North of the Val d'Isère and Tignes region are the third generation French resorts of La Plagne and Les Arcs in the Haute Savoie, just below Geneva. Altitudes from 3,800 ft to 10,000 ft.

Resorts
La Plagne has 8 villages: La Plagne itself, Plagne Villages, Aime-la-Plagne, Bellecote, and Belle Plagne in the mountains; and Champagny, Montchavin and Montalbert in the valley, each with a distinct atmosphere. Les Arcs consists of three villages known by their metric heights: 1600, 1800 and 2000 (4,800 ft, 5,400 ft and 6,000 ft). Skiing for the serious and not-so-serious. The La Plagne region has 65 lifts including 5 cable-cars, a gondola and 10 chair lifts; Tignes has 50 lifts.

Accommodation
Thousands of beds throughout the area. Excellent food and good disco night life.

Activities
Teaching concentrates on ski styles; also 'ski music and dream' lessons; hang gliding; cinemas, swimming pools, saunas, concerts.

difficult; a third as testing; half are easy. Between and around them stretch acres of unbeaten snow. A ten-mile run down 6,500 vertical feet is typical of the challenge provided by the slopes. There is also the quiet pleasure of skiing along easy runs between the villages. The not-so-serious skier can explore from restaurant to restaurant; there are forty of them in the villages and on the slopes and they cover every speciality from *couscous* to frogs legs; *raclette* to *mousseline*. Some are quietly sophisticated within the great apartment blocks; at others skiers sit outside shepherds' huts eating off rough wood tables in the sunshine.

Very close to this great complex of La Plagne – so close that it is possible to ski from one to the other, though politically there is no plan to join them yet –.lies the equally great complex of Les Arcs.

Arcs 1600, 1800 and 2000 are the result of a dream of a remarkable man, Robert Blanc. Before he died in 1979, killed by an avalanche in his beloved mountains, he saw many of his dreams come true and the work of development still continues. Born in the mountains, Robert Blanc wanted to build his ski resort to complement rather than disrupt the slopes. He persuaded a financier called Roger Godino to head a consortium, and a great architect called Taillefer to design buildings which hugged the contours of the slopes. Gradually, as pressure on space has increased, the buildings in the second and third villages (called 1800 and 2000 after their heights in meters) have grown upwards but always the feeling for contour and the need for sunshine has been considered.

As in La Plagne the villages are compact, many of their buildings are linked and shuttle buses travel along the mountain roads between them while skiers follow the lifts and pistes. Every ray of sunshine is caught on apartment balconies, mountain restaurants and terraces.

Again the concept of, 'relax and enjoy the vacation', is all that the skier need worry about. Learning became fun because Robert Blanc was joint inventor of the short ski method (called *ski evolutif* in France) so his pupils learn fast and easily on skis only 3 ft long, balancing without poles until they are confident enough to progress to longer skis. *Ski sauvage* (exploring off-piste) is a regular part of ski school, when the instructor leads his class off the beaten trails to picnic in sheltered sunny spots or in old huts hidden in the mountains.

Recently Les Arcs ski school have taken up every likely and unlikely variation of skiing. It offers mono-skiing (on a single ski), ski-surfing, ski-flying (with wings attached to the arms instead of poles), or just setting off down a stretch of prepared speed track while a built-in timing system ticks away the seconds, and providing a time to be set against those of other skiers or used as a standard to beat and beat again. Hang gliding is taught at Les Arcs; there are 'ski music and dream' lessons for those who like to swing down the slopes while a cassette recorder pours music into the ears. Inner skiing and freestyle can be learnt and there is an area set aside for powder skiing through the trees. The chutes provide the most expert skier with exhilarating descents down narrow *couloirs* of snow. In contrast the crosscountry and snowshoe trails wind gently through quiet forests. Children, of course, have their own nurseries and mini clubs.

Down in the valley lies the old town of Bourg St Maurice, linked to Les Arcs 1600 by cablecar and road. Its railway brings skiers from Paris and Geneva; its garages are expert in fitting chains to cars for the last lap up the mountain road; its clinic is specially equipped to cope with the skier who meets with an accident. Too low to be reliably linked by piste to the resorts above, it acts as a link with the outside world. Buses run from the station to Val d'Isère and Tignes as well as to La Plagne and the Three Valleys.

Les Arcs is for the skier who wants to experiment, whether it is equipment, technique or mountain scenery which attracts him. Only the safety of the skier is taken seriously; the piste preparation and security is meticulous, so all the skier has to do is enjoy himself.

All the hotel and apartment rooms at Les Arcs are provided with closed circuit radio and Radio-Arcs broadcasts every day in several languages. It tells what is on in the way of entertainment, which celebrities are visiting (for this is a smart French resort popular with film stars and cabinet ministers), what the weather is expected to do, and which areas will be the best to ski that day. Fun races, expeditions and special courses are described, so that anyone wishing to take part can do so.

These great skiing areas are the answer for those who think that skiing up and down a slope several times is boring. Within the huge ski areas there are limitless possibilities to explore. With the snow conditions changing every day according to the weather, and a vast area of mountain to cover, each morning and afternoon is a new experience. But as well as skiing there are gastronomic experiences, delicious food in old Savoyard huts (or in modern Mexican restaurants, or in Parisian gourmet surroundings). The shops combine the chic clothes of Paris with the carved wood and stones of the mountains. Movie houses, swimming pools, saunas, concerts and even amusement arcades provide even the most blasé teenager with continuous occupation.

Lunch on the
slopes at
Les Arcs

WHAT KIND OF SKIING

Driving

*S*ome of the great cities of the world have ski areas which can be reached in a few hours by the driver. New York, of course, is one, with Hunter Mountain to the North, cleverly covered with man made snow if nature does not do her job. The Norwegians, Finns and Swedes flood out of their cities to ski at weekends. Geneva has motorways radiating out to take its inhabitants swiftly to the mountains. So many drivers become day-skiers that resorts such as Flaine, in France, have special lifts built near car parks outside the village, so that the day-visitors can reach the main slopes without cluttering up the inner village lifts.

There are so many resorts, in both continents, within easy driving reach of one another that to take a car on vacation opens up a great variety of skiing. It also has the advantage that all sorts of treasures can be taken along – just in case they are needed. The agonizing choice of whether to put in an extra heavy anorak or another après-ski outfit is settled; both are put in the back of the car. Then if the resort originally chosen has no snow, everything is just packed back into the car and driven to wherever the snow is plentiful. Finally, from many homes, the cost of driving several people in one car is less than paying their fares by air or train.

Often it is cheaper to stay in a valley town than in a resort – prices tend to rise with altitude in the mountains. Valleys can be overcast while the mountaintops are sunny but the idea is to travel up to a nearby resort each day. True there is no après-ski atmosphere down in the towns at night but as a compensation the prices at the restaurants are usually much lower.

Martigny in Switzerland makes a good base, for it is within an hour-and-a-half's drive from a dozen different resorts. Verbier is the closest, just 16 miles South off the Grand St Bernard pass. If the lines are long there, the great ski area can be approached through nearby Haute Nendaz or Thyon 2000. In complete contrast is the little resort of

Ovronnez just across the Rhône Valley and, next to it, Anzère's big blocks of chalet-shaped apartments, and lifts going up towards the Wildhorn.

The old town of Sion is just 16 miles from Martigny through vineyard country and has an old Bishop's Palace perched on a hill in the center of the town. Up an easy road from Sion lies a long shelf with Crans, Montana, Vermala and Aminona facing south towards the mighty mountain range from the Matterhorn to Mont Blanc. Crans-Montana has a wide expanse of sunny intermediate skiing, and from Aminona there are lifts to the Plaine Morte glacier. Back down to Sion and further upstream along the Rhône, there is a turning off to Leukerbad, a name going back to the early days of skiing history. It grew up by a spa and although the resort has not developed greatly since then, there are lifts, and the famous hot springs are still there.

Still within reach of Martigny is the Saas valley running South from the Rhône. To visit Zermatt would, of course, entail leaving the car and taking the train, but Saas Fee allows drivers into a big car park on the edge of the village from which they can set off on foot to the lifts for the Langfluh, Felskinn, Plattjen or Hannig areas.

The next valley, traveling West now, is the Val d'Anniviers; old chalets and villages line the route up to Zinal. For centuries the people of this valley used to spend their winters down tending vines in the valley and with spring, move with their flocks to the alpine pastures in the mountains. Zinal, Grimentz and St Luc all have ski lifts and are worth a visit. Vercorin, again fairly limited but interesting to see, lies in the next valley.

With a car and so much variety it is not difficult to avoid crowds at weekends, choose the high glaciers if snow is short or keep down among the trees when blizzards threaten.

As an alternative to staying in one town and driving out from it each day, it is also possible to move slowly along a valley, staying each night in a different resort. The Simmental is a good example. It runs all the way from Spiez on Lake Thun to Saanen, where the road rises and divides to go over the Vaudois Alps either by the Col des Mosses or the Col du Pillon before coming down via Leysin to Aigle.

The whole valley is a limestone ridge with a fairly steep scarp to the South, but unlike granite mountains these are covered with short grass with no protruding rocks. This means that provided there is the thinnest layer of snow they are skiable. The only problem is when it finally gets so warm that bare muddy patches appear, to stop skiers in their tracks, but this rarely happens before late spring.

The driver might start at the old village of Zweisimmen where an excellent gondola leads up to the Rinderberg and a detour could be made one day to Lenk. Back on the main road Saanenmoser and Schönreid have lifts going up the Hornberg and Hornfluh and then comes the division of the road with a choice of routes. The northern road, over the Col des Mosses goes through Château d'Oex, where the daughters of the rich attend finishing schools. Col des Mosses itself has become a ski village. The southern route goes first through Gstaad, the chic home of princes, racing drivers and movie stars. The Col du Pillon can close, in particularly stormy weather, but just past it is Les

Diablerets where the lift goes high enough for summer skiing. Then as the two roads converge again there is a valley leading up to Leysin, where there is a mountaineering school, all the equipment to encourage freestylers, and big hotels for school groups.

The whole long valley is a paradise for the off-piste explorer. The mountains are dotted with trees and chalets on the lower slopes, giving way to the occasional hay-hut further up.

These are just two Swiss examples of a central town and a long valley which are worth exploring. They can be found in every country In France, the Mont Blanc area is rich with resorts. Chamonix has lifts rising from several spots round the town, each opening up a different ski area. A few miles towards the Swiss border there is Argentière and Col des Montets with great glacier slopes. Les Houches, St Gervais and Les Contamines each have their own character and Mégève still retains its atmosphere of prewar French chic. In contrast is the little-known Nôtre Dame de Bellecombe, where French parents bring their children for quiet family vacations.

In Austria the Europa Sportregion unites a group of resorts one of which is Zell-am-See, set out beside its beautiful lake. Kaprun, with its great summer skiing area on the Kitzsteinhorn lies close and also within easy driving distance are Wagrain, where Atomic skis are made, and St Johann-in-Pongau. Here a series of picturesque traditional Austrian villages are linked over the mountains which separate them by chairlifts and ski pistes. Down a southerly valley lie the quartet of Dorfgastein, Bad Hofgastein, Badgastein and Sportgastein. The first two are small ski villages; Badgastein is a famous old spa with turn-of-the-century hotels, a casino and a strong Edwardian flavor. Sportgastein in total contrast has recently been built on the slopes above. This is all good skiing country.

From Châtillon in the Aosta Valley of Italy, or its more elegant neighbor St Vincent, one could visit Cervinia and Val Tournanche just above; or the three Gressoney villages in the next valley. La Thuile opens up the beautiful touring country of the Gran Paradiso and Champoluc is only an hour away.

Many tour operators offer special packages for motorists, with self-catering accommodation included but this takes away the flexibility of moving from place to place. Many airlines offer fly-drive packages, which have the advantage that long journeys from home to the mountains are avoided but equally many of the reasons for driving are lost – packing is restricted and fares must be paid. Car hire, like gasoline, is relatively cheap in the United States but very expensive in Europe. As a result, most European drivers prefer to take their own cars.

It can be no fun to break down on a mountain pass in a blizzard, so it is worth giving the car a good check before leaving – especially the battery which gets a lot of work when heater, demister, lights and wipers are all used for long periods.

Good snow tires with plenty of tread are essential. Chains can be bought but unless the car is to be used very often on skiing trips it is usually better and cheaper to hire chains at mountainside garages when needed. There is no more maddening and mucky job than fitting chains on an open road and it is all too easy for the car to slide off a jack in deep snow. Road clearing is efficiently done in the mountains now, as resorts realize their livelihood depends on visitors being able to reach them easily, so it is rare for chains to be necessary, especially after the deep winter months have passed. Road reconstruction has insured that avalanche paths are diverted over the top of roads by tunnels and steep hairpins have been eased.

Both on motorways and in the mountains, windscreen wipers get a lot of use and lack of visibility is more often the reason for stationary cars than slippery road conditions. It is worth fitting new wipers before setting off and lifting them away from the screen when the car is standing in icy conditions. If they get iced onto the screen the rubber tears off. Special antifreeze is needed in the washer container or one spurt can cover the screen with a film of opaque ice.

Ski racks are made to many specifications. The best are those which hold skis inside their ski bags, for long journeys across salt-strewn roads and through the muddy mist thrown up by other traffic can clog bindings and rust the edges of skis. Unhappily in Europe skis and even ski racks can be stolen off the top of unattended cars, so the racks which lock onto the roof of a car at the same time as locking in the skis are best.

There are ski resorts – Isola near Nice is one – where the driver can take a course in ice driving. With famous rally drivers as instructors it can be exciting to spin a car deliberately, to slide it under control round an ice-covered course and to learn to predict just what will happen as adhesion deteriorates. Failing the chance to learn this way, an enthusiastic driver can take advantage of an empty car park after a cablecar station has closed. They make excellent skidpans and it is surprising how confidence and safety grow with experience. Both sudden breaking and jerky acceleration are avoided. Frontwheel drive is, of course, easier than rearwheel drive for control on steep uphill hairpins and fourwheel drive is best of all for the sort of rutted tracks that can be found in heavy snowfalls.

Cars often have to be parked on steep slopes in ski resorts and handbrakes tend to freeze on so it is best to park in gear. A ribbon tied to the handbrake is a reminder to the forgetful driver!

Most ski resorts are well equipped with convenient garages and underground parks. Indeed, the authorities take harsh measures against drivers who leave cars by the sides of roads, blocking the snow clearing equipment. Even so, a shovel can be useful to dig out a path for a blocked car and if a snow plough has smothered a car with snow it is as well to burrow a bit and make sure it is the right car that is being dug out before getting down to the job of shoveling.

One of the problems about icy roads is that they are not uniformly icy. Often a tree may spread a patch of shade across a road which has otherwise dried out in the sun. Or a stream may melt in the day time, trickle across a road and then freeze overnight to leave a treacherous patch. Drivers learn to look out for these traps. Notices by the sides of roads warn of falling stones but there is little a driver can do about them except look out for rocks which might puncture a sump, and avoid parking for a picnic just under a possible stonefall.

Buying a daypass or single lift ticket every day as one travels from resort to resort can be expensive but many places now sell area passes which cover whole regions.

The savings in taking a car are considerable. To fit four, or even three people with their baggage into a car is much cheaper than paying three or four fares, even when the cost of gas and road tolls have been taken into consideration. For those who are going out to their own self-catering accommodation, there is the advantage of carrying those foods which are cheaper at home, or which suit the family's taste. For those moving from resort to resort, lunch can be bought in the valley where paté, bread and fruit are considerably cheaper than meals bought on a mountainside.

SPAIN/ ANDORRA/ FRANCE

The Pyrenees

SPAIN/ANDORRA/FRANCE

The Pyrenees

La Molina   Baqueira Beret

Andorra   Barèges

La Mongie   St Lary

The old barrier of the Pyrenees proved formidable enough to split the great land masses of France and Spain, so that they grew into separate nations with quite different cultures. Yet the people who live in the mountains themselves are united by their politics, their language and their nature. To the West they are Basques, fierce in their resentment of government, whether it comes from Paris or Madrid. To the East they are Catalans, lighthearted and courteous, with innate hospitality. The Catalans welcome visitors and yet avoid being over commercial. After a few days vacation in the Pyrenees the visitor feels part of the life of the village.

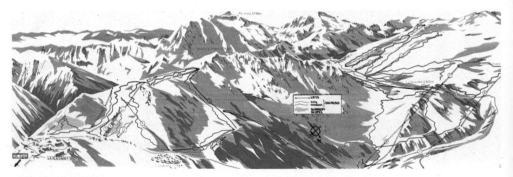

ST LARY SKI FACTS
Top station 7,319 ft / 1 cable car / 2 cabins /
5 chairs and 18 days / Maximum rise 2,760 ft /

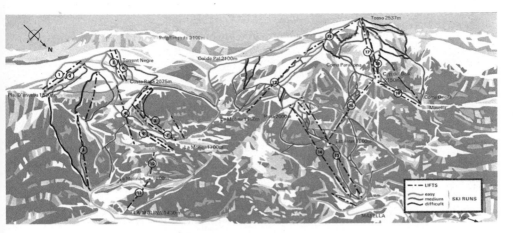

LA MOLINA SKI FACTS
Top station 8,315 ft / 10 chair lifts /
9 drag lifts / Maximum rise 3,106 ft /

BAREGES / LA MONGIE SKI FACTS
Top station 7,715 ft / 1 funicular / 1 cable car / 2 cabins /
1 basket lift / 8 chairs and 14 drags / Maximum rise 2,616 ft /

Low prices help to give the feeling that nobody is trying to make money out of the tourists and drink is particularly cheap, especially in duty free Andorra.

Reaching the villages can present problems. Barcelona and Zaragoza are the nearest airports to the Spanish resorts and Tarbes to the French. Long bus transfers are needed but no one can get bored watching the dramatic scenery through which the narrow roads wind. Within the resorts, waiting for the buses that are often needed to reach skilifts can be more frustrating, for the timetables, especially on the Spanish side, are frequently erratic and often do not exist.

Waiting for the lifts themselves is seldom a problem. Occasionally there are queues at weekends when people from the nearby towns come up for the day but generally the slopes are well able to cope with the number of visitors for which there are beds. February, when the French take their time off (French schools close either for the first or second two weeks of February) tends to fill the hotels, leaving the long sunny days of March as the best time for visitors.

The snow is affected by water-laden winds coming in from the Atlantic, particularly in the more westerly areas. This means more crust and ice than powder but it can also mean beautiful spring snow. There is excellent off-piste skiing to be explored in the Pyrenees, especially as the local people prefer the pistes, so the untracked snow remains in good condition.

Because the mountains are rolling rather than peaked, there are good crosscountry trails round most of the ski resorts. Ski jumping is also popular, so it does not require too much bravery to try a lesson or two on the specially small learners' jumps. Good instruction is given both for crosscountry and jumping.

One of the very first areas to be developed for skiing was La Molina in Spain. The Catalan Touring Club built a climbing hut on a slope above the railway at the turn of the century and ski-tourers began to use it as a base for their expeditions. Gradually the village developed up along a straggling mile-long road until recently Supermolina, with a first class hotel and modern apartment block was built at 5,210 ft. For a time La Molina and Supermolina struggled with separate lift systems and administrations but now they have united to the benefit of villagers and guests. The two have even linked with nearby La Masella, a purpose-built complex in the next valley which shares the same skiing area.

This is the biggest skiing area in Spain, served by 21 lifts which link 43 miles of pistes. La Tossa is the highest point at 8,370 ft from which many runs return to Supermolina or Masella. Those to Masella are cut down wide pistes through forests, but towards Supermolina the trees grow sparsely over the slopes. There is plenty of variety in runs above the tree line and down narrow gullies. So long as snow conditions allow, it is possible to ski down to the railway from which chair lifts come up again at the back of the village to Supermolina.

The hotels vary from simple to luxurious and they take it in turn to put on some kind of entertainment at night, in which the ski school often gets involved. Carnival (which in Catholic Spain stretches flexibly into Lent) makes a good excuse for evenings of dressing up, processions and parties.

Another big skiing area on the Spanish side of the Pyrenees is Baqueira Beret, where King Juan-Carlos is often to be seen on the slopes. Near the old town of Viella, Baqueira Beret has 15 lifts in a very well planned system rising to 8,067 ft. From this height there is a particularly testing run down Escornicrabes to the valley of Orri at 6,100 ft but there is also plenty of intermediate skiing. Of all the Pyrenean resorts, Baqueira is the most tightly organized and professionally marketed. Perhaps it owes this to its links with Vail for the two resorts are twinned.

Baqueira is relatively new but seven miles away is the old town of Viella with stone walls and attractive slate-roofed houses. On the outskirts of Viella, the La Tuca complex has been built close to a series

FACTS

Location
Mountain range of South West Europe, separating the Iberian peninsula from France. The highest peaks are Aneto (11,168 ft) and Posets (11,047 ft) but the altitudes in the ski areas do not go beyond 9,500 ft.

Ski areas
Spain: La Molina and Supermolina, served by over 20 lifts (rising to La Tossa at 8,370 ft); Baqueira Beret, (served by 15 lifts) (rising to 8,069 ft). *Andorra:* Soldeu, Pas de la Casa. *France:* Barèges, La Mongie (served by 45 lifts) (rising to Pic du Midi at 9,500 ft), and St Lary (rising to La Tourette at 7,650 ft).

Accommodation
This ranges from the developed resorts, where there is a variety of hotels and apartments, to barely developed villages best visited for the day.

Activities
In addition to downhill skiing, there are fine crosscountry trails and a strong local interest in ski jumping; thermal waters at Barèges.

of chair lifts which rise above the treeline to some good short steep slopes.

Andorra grew out of the old medieval bishopric of Urgell. Thanks to its independence it offers a great range of duty free goods which attract weekend crowds. There are two main ski areas, Soldeu and Pas de la Casa, the first of which is tiny. There are only 250 tourist beds in Soldeu but skiers come in by bus from Arinsal and La Massana nearby where there are a less extensive network of lifts and less reliable snow. Runs are mostly cut through the trees and can get cold and icy.

The Pas de la Casa/Grau Roig area is only 20 minutes away by bus. Because it balances on the French and Spanish borders, skiers from both countries visit it. The runs are fairly short and easy.

Barèges and La Mongie are French, set in the Atlantic Pyrenees and reached via Tarbes airport. They share 50 miles of pistes covered by 45 linked lifts on a single liftpass with a capacity for 20,000 skiers an hour. The whole area is a paradise for the beginner-to-intermediate skier who enjoys long runs. Some pistes reach as far as ten miles.

Barèges has thermal waters to bathe away the aches after an energetic day. La Mongie was built for skiing after a cablecar up to an observatory on the nearby Pic du Midi (9,500 ft) began to be used in winter by skiers. Tourmalet is a big complex on the outskirts of La Mongie which brings its capacity up to 5,000 beds.

Another French resort reached via Tarbes is St Lary. The old village at 2,750 ft bustles with small shops and bars but a cablecar to Pla d'Adet 3,000 ft up reveals the skiing area. From here lifts, pistes and a road link with Espiaube further along the shelf from which a gondola goes up to La Tourette at 7,650 ft. The area is good for beginners and intermediates and suits families in an unsophisticated way.

Formigal, Cauterets and La Gourette are amongst the many other villages being developed in the Pyrenees and if the roads were better it would be an ideal area to explore by car. As it is, there is plenty of skiing in any of the big areas to satisfy a fairly good skier and there are some occasional long or difficult runs to be explored.

The late hours common in Spain percolate through to all the region and add to the feeling of relaxation. Winter sunset does not come too early in these southern latitudes and when it does, there is still time for a siesta before dinner and the serious business of testing the Spanish brandy. Even the mountains seem to stretch out sleepily rather than crowding overhead in great peaks and the altitudes are too moderate to prevent sleep. The sun shines often and the friendliness of the local people makes a perfect background to a restful holiday.

Ski school on
the Milky way
in Italy

ITALY

Piedmont and the Milky Way

The Dolomites

Piedmont and the Milky Way

maps
page 72

Saulx d'Oulx Sestrière Clavière
Sansicario Montgenevre

West of Turin, towards the border with France, there is an area of Alps once ruled by the old Kings of Savoy, which lends itself to skiing. Sestrière, on a pass just an hour from the city, was built in the thirties; Sauze d'Oulx rose to be the mecca of the young in the sixties; Sansicario is modern and the lifts and pistes which stretch on out to the old border villages of Clavière and Montgenèvre have only recently been linked together under the name of the Milky Way. The sun shines here with Mediterrannean warmth but the energy and organization which has gone into its development come from the clear-headed, hard working northern Italian industrialists rather than their *dolce-far-niente* compatriots of the South.

Sestrière was developed by Fiat before the Second World War and they had it designed with the panache of a *gran turismo* car. The round tower hotels, Ducchi d'Aosta and Torre, surprised and delighted the smart young skiers of the day. At the center of each is a continuous circular ramp with bedrooms and suites radiating out from it. Prewar parties used to include an orange-rolling race down the ramps, ending in the stair wells.

For the aristocrats there was the Principe di Piemonte hotel, built like Sleeping Beauty's palace and like it, hidden among the trees with its own long driveway. Set apart from the village, it had a private skilift so that its guests could join the main network. The heated outside pool was one of the first to be seen in a ski resort.

Good mountain slopes, easy access and efficient organisation made Sestrière the Italian choice for the fashionable Arlberg-Kandahar race. Publicity and consequent crowds led to an extension to the lift system. Three main areas set round the snowy bowl which surrounds Sestrière each have their own cablecars; Fraiteve, Banchetta and Alpette/Sises can absorb a vast number of skiers.

After the war, ski resorts had to spread their appeal further than the very rich. Club Mediterrannée took over the round tower hotels, and big car parks catered for those who drove up from Turin on Saturdays and Sundays. The resort has remained popular, and big new developments are now planned.

Over the mountain to the North, Sauze d'Oulx grew quickly from the middle sixties to become a seething, swinging center, particularly attractive to young English-speaking package groups. The resort is excellent for the first-time skier in his or her late teens or early twenties. The compact, busy village, half old half new, has nursery slopes near the center as well as half-way up the mountain. All the instructors speak English and they take the dashing, enjoy-yourself attitude of the lighthearted Italian Romeo rather than the serious improve-your-technique approach of more northern schools.

At night five discos keep the tempo throbbing, helped by cheap Italian wine and heady grappa. Young crowds pack into the many restaurants and bars. *Pensions* produce the traditional pasta and pizzas, while big hotels such as the Palazza cook Italian food at its delicate best. Small strong black coffees clear heads in time to set off and ski next morning.

Sauze has two satellites, a small settlement up on Sportinia, the first lift station, at 7,000 ft and Jouvenceaux, an outlying village just below old Sauze. There are plenty of intermediate slopes among the trees and the sunny atmosphere gives just the right background to a first ski vacation. It is usually possible to ski between Sauze and Sestrière, though a guide is essential. The liftpasses are interchangeable though a supplement is needed to qualify Sauze's skiers to use the rest of the Milky Way system.

The building of Sansicario made possible the linking of Sestrière with Montgenèvre to form the Milky Way. This great chain of lifts, covered by a pass that includes 200 miles of pistes, stretches from Borgata Sestrière (East of the main village), through Sansicario and Cesana on to Clavière and Montgenèvre to the West in France.

The Italians call Sansicario a 'fourth generation' resort, claiming that it has all the advantages of the third-generation French stations with the extra dimensions of natural mountain architecture, and summer as well as winter facilities. It allows cars only as far as covered parks outside the village and its builders follow a plan of grey stone-clad chalets, not more than three stories in height. At 5,600 ft it is fairly snowsure. Down from Fraitève on the Sestrière side there is a good black run. Widely spaced larch trees are fun to swoop through when the powder falls; and there are some easy runs, though the nursery slopes are a few minutes walk from the village. In Sansicario, the evenings are quiet. This is an area for families, racers and those skiers who want to travel for miles during the day rather than dancing for hours during the night.

If Sansicario is new, then Cesana is old. On the crossroads for the mountain passes over by Sestrière and Montgenèvre, Cesana has kept all the character of a little old mountain market town. Clavière, next village on the Milky Way, lies right on the French border – the customs

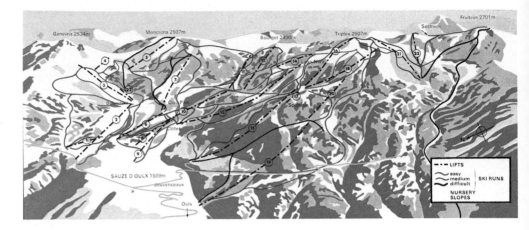

SAUZE D'OULX SKI FACTS
Top station 8,220 ft / 1 bucket lift / 6 chairs /
16 drags / Maximum rise 2,289 ft /

MONTGENEVRE / **CLAVIERE** SKI FACTS
Top station 8,832 ft / 1 cabin / 7 chairs /
19 drags / Maximum rise 1,602 ft /

---

post goes across the main street, though no one is likely to be held up
for want of a passport. There are easy glades through the trees, as well
as some steep ones; the runs themselves are not long as this is only a
part of the much bigger system.

Montgenèvre is, of course, just in France but it is as Italian as
spaghetti. Turin is only sixty miles away while Grenoble is more like
ninety and there are several popular French ski resorts to tempt the
French from Grenoble before they ever reach Montgenèvre. The long
village runs East West and the valley is wide and sunny. It has two
compact lift systems of its own, one sunny and South-facing, the other
North and snowsure until late spring.

Not just one vacation but a whole series could be spent in the
Piedmont area. A start could be made in Sauze where slopes and ski
school bring beginners confidently onto their skis, while the nightlife

helps them forget the occasional bruise. Sansicario is the best central point on the Milky Way for anyone who wants to explore far and wide. Clavière and Montgenèvre are inexpensive and have their own short and varied slopes. Those who want some sophistication, will find it at Sestrière, as well as a wide, well kept ski area.

Italy's financial problems may have slowed down development but they cannot close the excellent mountain ranges. They cannot take away the pleasure of sitting in the warm sun and enjoying the Val d'Ostana cheese and ham flavored dishes. Meanwhile the industrious Piedmontese are building new resorts and setting up new lift systems, just as they have been doing for generations.

FACTS

Location	Resorts	Accommodation	Activities
West of Turin and touching the French borders is the Piedmont area in the Italian Alps, South of the French resorts of Val d'Isère and Tignes.	Sestrière (5,555 ft), covering the ski areas of Fraitève, Banchetta and Alpette/Sises, a luxury resort built in the 30s; Sauze d'Oulx (rising to Sportinia at 7,000 ft), developed in the 1960s; Sansicario (5,600 ft), a 'fourth generation' resort; Clavière and Montgenèvre. 25 lifts in Sauze, 30 throughout the Milky Way.	From the great 1930s hotels of Sestrière to the *pensions* and family hotels of Sauze d'Oulx and Sansicario; entertainment follows the same pattern: discos in Sauze d'Oulx, quiet in Sansicario.	Emphasis on skiing and learning to ski, and the region is ideal for beginners looking for an inexpensive, unsophisticated but fun-loving introduction to the sport. Summer skiing in Sansicario.

ITALY

The Dolomites

Cortina d'Ampezzo

map *page 76*

Italians have taken downhill skiing to their hearts and, because they love it themselves, much of their enthusiasm rubs off on the people who visit their country for holidays. The whole Dolomite area up in the North East corner of Italy is dotted with ski resorts. And, a miracle of organization, the lift system is computerised, so that one plastic pass card can be used in 44 different resorts. The card is pushed through a scanner, which opens a gate to let the skier onto a lift and at the same time records a point. All the points are collected and the lift owners paid accordingly. This cuts out all the fighting which so often breaks out between other adjoining ski resorts over dividing the lift revenue.

This Superski Dolomiti liftpass certainly helps the skier by linking the many resorts and also gives a great advantage to the driver. Dozens of small resorts within easy reach by car, and no time (or money) is wasted buying a new ticket for each area. When calculated in lire per square mile, it must offer the cheapest skiing in the world.

The coordination of the lifts is not quite as superbly organized. Often the top of.one lift does not quite reach the bottom of the next, necessitating an undignified scramble over a narrow bit of icy path. However, there is a generous supply of cafés dotted across the slopes of the Dolomites, giving every encouragement to those who want to rest in the sun and sip a *cappucino*.

The Dolomites are unlike mountains anywhere else in the world. Instead of peaks and cols they have great cliff walls rising to a high ragged plateau. The red magnesian limestone stands like a reef between the blue of the sky and the white snow below.

At the base of the cliffs, yet still high in the mountains, are gently undulating, open slopes which are a joy for beginners. They can take a cablecar from the valley, ski up in the sunshine and not feel that, just because they are inexpert, they are confined to the valley floor. They may need to take the cablecar down again at the end of the day, for the section between the rolling uplands and the villages is often steep, with pistes chopped out of dense forests. These are the domain of the better skiers and they also make excellent race courses.

The Dolomites cover a huge area from Plan de Corones in the North to San Martino di Castrozza in the South; from Bolzano in the West to Cortina in the East. At their heart, just to the East of Bolzano, lies the great Sella massif. This block of mountains is surrounded by old pass roads which link dozens of traditional old villages. A famous circuit which can be completed in a day by a competent skier, goes up the lifts and down the pistes right round the Sella. It needs some planning to catch the lifts when there are no queues at the bottlenecks; and with thousands of vertical feet of skiing, some stamina is required but there are no really difficult stretches. There is a great feeling of achievement which.comes from traveling over so much country, past so many different villages. Selva, San Cassiano, Corvara, Colfosco, there is a great choice of places to stay along the circuit.

To the North of the Sella Ronda, there is what amounts to a miniature replica round a mountaintop called Plan de Corones (Kronplatz). Not majestic like the Sella but more like a pudding basin, it has a ring of villages around its base, like Riscone, San Vigilio and Valdaora. There are slopes steep enough for the Italian team to train here but, again, easy country on top.

The language of the Dolomites is German, for it was part of the Austro-Hungarian Empire for centuries. Every village has its German name. It can be confusing to find Selva referred to as Wolkenstein or Riscone as Reischach, but tradition dies hard in the mountains. Fortunately a good deal of autonomy has now been granted to the region, so there is no longer any need to fear riots from local patriots. The castles perched on every vantage point are picturesque reminders of ancient wars.

The Dolomites do, of course, have a fashionable resort, and it is a very beautiful one. Cortina lies in a bowl surrounded by fabulous mountain scenery. As cablecars rise on every side of the town, the best

---

FACTS

Location
The Dolomite range, or Alpi Dolomiti, is the dramatic mountain range characterised by great cliff walls and plateaus in the Trentino region of North East Italy. The prevailing language is German.

Ski areas
Ski areas and lift systems are dotted throughout the Dolomites; the principal centers are the Sella Massif, east of Bolzano, surrounded by villages like Selva, San Cassiano, Corvara and Colfosco; and Plan de Corones to the North of Sella Ronda, with the villages of Riscone, San Vigilio and Valdaora. The most fully developed resort, with good night life, accommodation and shopping, is Cortina d'Ampezzo (8,000 ft). Cortina boasts 48 lifts, including 6 cables, a gondola and 15 chair lifts, and the best ski school in Italy.

Lifts C = Cable Car D = Drag lift CH = Chair lift G = Gondola
Ski Runs Very easy——— Medium ——— Difficult ———

Cortina d'Ampezzo

CORTINA D'AMPEZZO SKI FACTS
Top station 11,246 ft / 6 cable cars / 1 cabin /
15 chairs / 21 drags / Maximum rise 2,531 ft /

conditions of snow can be enjoyed whatever the season. In spite of its size, Cortina remains attractive, with a high-spired church and old stone buildings.

Italians tend to rise late in Cortina, take a cablecar for a few runs in the morning and settle to a leisurely lunch in one of the many panoramic restaurants. During the siesta hours they sit on the terraces and deepen their tans in the strong Italian sun. Then it is time to ski back to the town and change into furs for a stroll through the exotic shopping streets. Dinner follows, perhaps at El Toulas or la Caponnina del Boite and the night comes to a lively end at the Bilbo or Tiger discos.

The Dolomites also cater for the toughest travelers. School groups are brought to its small villages, packed into bunk rooms, fed on spaghetti and Italian ice cream and infected for the rest of their lives with the Italians enthusiasm for skiing.

The appeal of the Dolomites is, more than to anyone else, to the explorer. Explorers may not be superb skiers but people who want to travel from village to village, either driving to a new lift each day or simply setting off on skis in a different direction in this superb traveling terrain.

WHAT KIND OF SKIING

Ski touring

Skiing for some people is the fun of an easy dash down a prepared piste, the thrill of striving to go faster down beaten pistes surrounded by darting, bright-colored figures; joining the noisy crowd on the terrace of the mountain restaurant for lunch and then linking turns down a mogul slope to the beat of music pouring out of lift-top loud speakers.

For tourers the essence of the mountains lies in silence and stillness.

Skitouring in Switzerland
Swiss National Tourist Office

Satisfaction comes from finding a way through many dangers to the splendor of the mountain peaks and from the companionship of a small group of people sharing the effort, the beauty and the achievement.

Driving along mountain highways and seeing the signposts advertising ski resorts up every branching valley road, it seems as if the mountains must be covered with lifts. Certainly conservationists battle to stop the building as if there were no wilderness left in the world. Yet, when flying across the same mountains, it is obvious that only a tiny percentage of even the most developed areas of the world is regularly invaded by skiers. What remains is the tourers' paradise.

Part of the satisfaction of touring lies in asceticism. Lungs and muscles are stretched when traveling across the mountains without the help of lifts, and the knowledge needed to find the right route through the best snow only builds with experience. For an inexperienced skier to go just a few yards away from a 10,000 ft cablecar station and set off on an unmarked route without a guide is as sensible as jumping out of a plane at 10,000 ft without a parachute.

It is easy to start touring with a group of experienced friends or with a ski school class which is taking a day off from the pistes, picnicking for lunch and returning in the evening to the comfort of the resort. Once crossing powder, crust and heavy snow become an interesting challenge rather than a disaster, longer tours can lead to days traveling across the mountains from hut to hut, or using one as a base from which to explore the surrounding range and climb neighboring peaks.

The fascination of snow craft lies in the infinite ways the intricate white crystals can change. They knit together, are blown by wind, melt into water, harden to ice and soften again in the sun. Every change alters the quality of the snow over which the tourer skis; the challenge of touring is to find the best possible conditions whatever the weather and to escape from the very real traps which the mountains lay for their invaders.

Snow does not usually fall in extremely low temperatures. While it falls the fresh powder is pleasant to ski through, even if visibility is difficult. If very low temperatures follow, the snow becomes light and fluffy, flowing up round the skier who is in a state of breathtaking exhilaration. Some fortunate areas, such as the Rocky Mountains of Utah enjoy this kind of snow even as it falls, for the clouds have come high across the deserts of California and the crystals have freeze-dried on their way.

Once temperatures rise, snow softens and knits together, becoming heavier to move through. If this wet snow freezes overnight it forms a crust which can break under a skier's weight to make turning difficult. Or it can form a thicker crust of ice to ski over next morning. Sometimes sun melts the top of a thick crust and makes one of the easiest surfaces over which to ski – spring snow.

Wind can also pack the snow hard as it falls, so that it forms wind crust, or juts out over the leeside of ridges to form cornices which can break under the weight of an unwary skier. Glaciers form cracks across their flow as they make their slow progress down mountainsides. Often these cannot be seen from above, but they are usually covered with fragile snowbridges, again ready to trap an inexperienced skier.

Snow is laid down in layers and each layer differs in structure according to the temperature and wind which prevail before the next snowfall. A layer packed down hard by the wind lies over another which has a thin crust over powder; the most dangerous layers turn to smooth icy granules which can act like a carpet of ball bearings over which, weeks later, the upper layers can slide. Unless the tourer knows the weather history of each slope over which he skis, he cannot tell if it will slide. Even those who love and know the mountains best often get trapped by avalanches, but choosing the right contour, the right orientation, even the right time of day to tackle a potential avalanche slope will always reduce the danger.

Special equipment makes touring easier. Skis are generally shorter, broader and softer than those used on the piste, so that they turn more easily in heavy snow and are light for climbing. Ski mountaineers even have a hole in the front of their skis or a rope to be threaded through so that the skis can be hauled up rock faces. Often they are painted bright orange for eacy identification in bad visibility.

At one time seal skins were tied to the base of skis, so that forward sliding was easy but the fur acted as a brake to stop skis sliding back on an upward slope. Most tourers now use strips of manmade fibers which act in the same way and can be stuck on or peeled off as needed.

Boots are softer than those used on the piste and made for climbing as well as skiing. Bindings allow the heel of the boot to lift, which makes walking far less tiring. They often get very complicated as they must also clamp down for ordinary skiing, and include a safety release. Crampons or *Harscheisen* can be attached under the boot or ski to grip into the ice when crossing a slippery slope.

Many thin layers of clothing are better than a few very heavy ones, and modern insulating fibers keep the heat in well when required and can be made with plenty of zips to open and let air in when climbing.

All sorts of minor equipment becomes essential in the mountains where there is no mountaintop shop ready to supply sunburn cream or goggles, and a rucksack is standard equipment to carry first aid, knife, torch, whistle, shovel, etc.

The most essential equipment of all is a radio transceiver, which must be strapped onto every member of a group. These emit and pick up bleeps, so speeding up the location of anyone buried by an avalanche. Time in digging out a buried skier can be vital.

All this equipment makes for heavy packs in the mountains, especially if the group is not returning to the valley at night but staying in a mountain hut.

Most of the huts were built by alpine clubs and, compared with hotels, their accommodation is basic, but when the alternative is digging a snowhole and sleeping in it they seem positively luxurious. Beds consist of long wooden shelves – *Matrazenlager* – along which the sleepers lie, each wrapped in a blanket with a pillow underhead. The only water available is melted snow, so washing is kept to a minimum and the lavatory usually consists of a hut perched over a precipice.

Some huts have guardians, who will provide an evening meal; for others tourers must bring their own food, though supplies are often stocked up in the summer. On some of the better known routes across the mountains the huts, even though capable of sleeping 100 skiers get crowded over the holidays and must be booked in advance.

Early hours are kept in the huts for the snow is at its best – and safest – early in the day when the temperatures are low. Planning to reach a destination long before nightfall also gives leeway in case of accidents, mistaken routes or difficult weather. So by 4 am the huts are astir with skiers drinking their coffee, repacking their rucksacks and setting off.

Now the guide shows his skill as the group traverses the contours, coming down in the shadow of big peaks where the cold has kept the powder light or finding spring slopes where the sun has had its effect. There are long empty slopes down which to cut fresh tracks, time to enjoy the awesome beauty of the surrounding ranges, perhaps a peak to climb which gives a view of white-capped ridges marching away to the horizon.

By early afternoon the hut for the next night must be within reach, for avalanches become more likely as the temperature rises and the snow softens. The best of the day's snow conditions are over and this is the time to relax in the hut, get out the maps and study the route for the next day. The weather forecast is heard, reports from groups coming into the hut from other directions are considered. The day's events are talked over in the easy companionship of other tourers.

These are the rewards for the efforts of climbing, the thirst and difficult breathing in the thin air of high altitudes. Tourers have no hesitation in suffering this for the supreme satisfaction of tracing a path through the silent mountains, the feeling of surviving on top of the world through their own efforts.

There are schools to which tourers can go to learn their craft. The Alpine Sportschule Andermatt is particularly famous. Martin Epp, its director, has ranged over the mountains of the world, especially the Rockies, and enjoys handing on their secrets to those who love the mountains. There are weekly courses for all standards from the beginner to the high alpinist, at which the tourer can practise among experts and learn snowcraft, mountaineering and an appreciation of the beauty of the peaks.

WHAT KIND OF SKIING

Crosscountry

Langlauf has
become a
fast-growing
alternative to
downhill

Today, when jogging is such a fashionable way to keep fit, there is an extra satisfaction in crosscountry skiing. On foot, the runner's efforts take him from stride to stride; on ski each stride is lengthened by a slide over the snow, so that ground is covered twice as fast – or half as energetically.

The technique is easily learnt. Right arm and left foot swing forward together, then left arm and right foot. The diagonal thrust gives both balance and momentum.

Crosscountry is not just a modern health fad. The first known ski was dug out of a bog in Sweden where it was used about 2,500 BC. In those days the only way to get about in winter was to put something under the feet to prevent them sinking into the snow.

In 1205 a two-year-old prince was rescued from rebels by two Norwegians and carried on skis to safety. The child grew up to be King Hakon, founder of Norway's greatness, and the Norwegian Ski Association still runs an annual race called Birkenbeiner after the rescuers to commemorate their bravery. Similarly, the Vasa race in Sweden commemorates a royal chase which took place in 1520 and the founding of a great Swedish dynasty. Now the Vasa attracts as many as 12,000 competitors who cover a distance of 50 miles.

This kind of mass crosscountry racing has spread all over the world. The 34 mile Wisconsin Birkebeiner races, the Rivière Rouge in Quebec and the Engadine Ski Marathon past St Moritz in Switzerland all attract tens of thousands of competitors. There is even a European league in which competitors build up points in five countries. The Va.a is one of the qualifying races, others are the Marcialonga (Italy), the Dolomiti (Austria), König Ludwig (Germany) and Finlandia.

Crosscountry racing looks and is energetic; it requires stamina and technique. But crosscountry skiing can be as gentle as the skier wishes. Nearly all ski resorts now prepare crosscountry trails and they start with simple loops just over one mile long. A notice at the start of the trail gives its length, so that day by day the distance can be built up to 3, 6, 16 or 25 miles. Prepared trails have pairs of ski-tracks pressed into them by machine. At least two pairs are laid alongside, to allow for easy overtaking and also to let crosscountry skiers travel amicably together. Unlike the breathless dash of downhill skiing, crosscountry is a sociable sport with time to talk. Modern trails often have cafés set conveniently beside them.

Unless an out-of-condition skier attempts to go too fast or too far, there is little chance of getting hurt while crosscountry skiing and every opportunity to build up health and strength.

Equipment is cheaper and more comfortable than that needed for downhill skiing. Skis are long but thin and light. The modern ones, made of glassfiber are easy to control and although those used by racers have to be very narrow to save weight, the beginner can balance quite easily on a suitable four-inch-wide ski. Boots are soft, light and flexible, reaching just ankle height in contrast to the high rigid sheaths needed for downhill. The binding attaches the toe of the boot to the ski, leaving the heel free to lift right up. Sticks are long and light. The emphasis in clothing is on several warm light layers covered with a light but breathing waterproof material.

Beginners need to keep to prepared trails and, before choosing a resort for crosscountry, it is as well to make sure that these run through pleasant country away from roads. The best are woodland paths in remote little valleys where birds and squirrels are the only other living beings and the trail wanders beside streams. All this is far from the hurlyburly of the crowded downhill pistes; there is no waiting for lifts and no expensive lift passes to buy.

Seefeld in Austria is surrounded by just such pleasant valleys and, as they progress, skiers can graduate to the ultimate in difficulty, the famous Olympic runs. There are excellent crosscountry schools in Austria which start pupils on flat fields and take them gradually over more difficult terrain until they can climb and descend quite steep slopes. As the crosscountry ski is unattached at the heel it is more difficult to control when turning downhill than an alpine ski but the technique is still learnt in a matter of hours.

Another natural starting point is Scandinavia, the home of crosscountry skiing, which has given the name *loipe* to trails all over the world. Hundreds of Norwegians pour out of the towns at weekends to huts in the forests near small towns like Morgedal and Norefjell. Here they live simply, buying their food and fuel at local depots and cooking for themselves. Norwegians make their outings family affairs. Father tows the baby, tucked into its own little sledge called a *pulka*; bigger children ski alongside and often the dog comes too.

The frozen lakes of Finland provide marvellously even tracks. Finland is so vast and its population so small that it is possible to ski away from a hotel and know that there is no human habitation for miles ahead.

In Canada the trapper trails round the St Laurence estuary take weekend skiers along streams by beaver dams and up into the hills. Guest ranches in the mountain parks of Banff, Jasper and Waterton Lakes in Alberta provide home coiking and a country atmosphere as a background to family crosscountry holidays. Far to the North West, Yukon's Whitehorse trails are cut through a landscape of blue-white mountain peaks where skiers cast long shadows in the shortlived sunlight.

In the United States, at the northern tip of the Appalachian chain, the great rolling Adirondacks have been fiercely protected against exploitation. Mountain lodges welcome guests and guide them on two, three- or five-day trails picnicking at lunchtime and sleeping in bunk beds. Across in the Rockies the touring centers are more sophisticated and tours into the High Uintas of Utah combine high Alpine bowls with featherlight powder snow.

The trails of the wilderness areas need careful planning and preparation. Many of them have boxes at the trail head in which the skier posts a note of his intended route. He can then be found in case of accident or bad weather. A whistle, a mirror for signaling and a windproof plastic bag in which to sleep are all sensible emergency equipment. Matches, a knife, first aid kit and ski repair kit are useful and no skier should go out without extra layers of light warm clothing, snacks which will not freeze and if possible a thermos of hot drink.

A skier able to tackle such country will have learnt the mysteries of waxing. There is a great art in applying the correct wax to the sole of a ski to enable it to slide forward smoothly, yet grip on upward tracks. A change in temperature will often require a change of wax, though modern waxes are becoming more adaptable. Modern skis, too, are constructed with overlapping scales on the soles, so that they slide forward but grip when going uphill.

Another joy of crosscountry is to travel with map and compass across untracked country. Along the border between France and Switzerland lie the Jura mountains and this long, low ridge makes perfect touring country. The Mont d'Or region in the center of France is also hospitable country for crosscountry tourers who plan their route from one comfortable inn to another. In the South East corner of Germany the little town of Zwiesel lies in the midst of a web of tracks along gentle ridges. A good map reader can make his way crosscountry from village to village along the contours and through the sparse woods. For those who lead sedantary, stressful city lives a crosscountry vacation provides true recreation.

map *page 88*

WHAT KIND OF SKIING

Summer skiing

Bormio   Zermatt   Kaprun

Val d'Isère   Mount Bachelor

Whistler   Squaw Valley

Arapahoe Basin   Mount Hood

Mammoth Mountain

*S*kiing is so much a winter activity that it may seem crazy to pursue it in summer but June to September can be the best months of all in the mountains. Up on the glaciers the sun beats out of a dark blue sky on perpetual snow. Down in the valleys golf courses and tennis courts emerge from their winter covers and resorts adapt themselves to dozens of summer occupations.

To travel up to the ski slopes in June is to go backwards in time from summer to winter. Down in the valleys the bees hum in the cherry blossom; from the root stocks of the vines long tendrils twine around the trellisses, covering them with broad green leaves. Further up the slopes the fruit trees give way to alpine meadows full of long grass and wild flowers: arnica, tsanteleina, harebell and rockrose then gentian, edelweiss and finally, when pockets of snow are appearing where the sun never reaches, the banks between are yellow with the wild crocus of early spring.

Those who have seen ski resorts only in winter are surprised when they find the stark black and white outlines softened by color. Granite-chip paths are edged with grass; between chalets appear garden plots neatly lined with vegetables while out over the balconies pour cascades of geraniums and petunias.

In summer, skiing is possible usually only in the mornings, for as the sun rises it gradually softens the overnight ice to spring snow, then breaks through the crust and finally turns it to slush. In most places by midday it is time to come down for lunch and decide what else to do with the day.

There are two quite different approaches to a summer skiing vacation. One is for the sybarite, the skier who wants to enjoy gentle glacier slopes in the morning, then make up for an early start by sleeping away the afternoons by a lake or pool, slipping into the water when the heat gets too strong; then spending the evening in tennis, minigolf or sightseeing.

Serious sportsmen occupy their time quite differently. They are in the Italian mountains, for example, to improve race techniques, to keep fit and to prepare for the competitive season ahead. Gymnastics start the day early, followed by training through slalom poles. After a swim in the afternoon there are more strenuous sports, running zigzag down the mountains perhaps – and up again. In the evening, video gives a record of what progress has been made, or there are lectures and movies.

For these skiers, there is an adventurous start to the day every morning, when a fleet of buses takes them from Bormio to the Stelvio Pass. The 35 minute journey is along a steep, winding, multi-hairpin road which is an engineering feat in itself. On the pass the lifts go up to nearly 12,000 ft, mostly over fairly easy terrain.

Bormio is an ancient Roman town built over thermal springs, with plenty to offer the sybarite too. The town was built on the busy trade route between Venice and the cities of Germany. Much of its old walls still stands, and of the dozens of churches, many add a touch of culture to a sporting vacation, like San Vitale, which was founded in the 12th century, and Crocefisso, which is decorated with 15th and 16th century frescoes. Nearby Livigno is worth visiting too. This lies in a duty free zone on the borders of Italy and Switzerland. Its long straggly main street is lined with shops selling drink, watches and cameras at amazingly low prices.

Moving into Switzerland, Zermatt has always been a good summer skiing area but it is now even better since the Klein Matterhorn lift was built. This reaches up to 12,530 ft and the ride needs a steady head for the cablecar goes straight up the sheer face of a cliff. The immense area with a choice of 19 tows is worth a brief attack of vertigo. And nearby is Plateau Rosa, linked with Cervinia, with pistes running down from 11,400 ft.

Zermatt is a delight in summer. There are plenty of tough mountaineers in the old streets with their ropes, pitons and iceaxes but the atmosphere is altogether more leisurely than in the winter months.

Over eastwards on the Brenner Pass between Innsbruck and the Dolomites lies Neustift, in Austria. Summer skiers find Neustift a good base from which to ski on the Stubai glacier where two gondolas, a chairlift and six tows cover six square miles of slopes. Freestylers practise up here in summer, twisting and turning as they leap off the snowy jumps and spending the afternoons trying out their more dangerous maneuvers in the specially aerated water of the swimming pools, that makes landing softer.

The Col de l'Iseran is one of the highest road passes in Europe and from Val d'Isère, in France, there is excellent summer skiing on the Grand Pissaillas. There are steep slopes between 10,375 ft and 12,500 ft where racers practise slaloming. The wide open spaces on Pont des Neiges and the Prariond are at the same altitude, with a descent of 550 ft for free skiing. Two chair lifts and six tows operate from 7.45 am to 12.45 pm every day through July and August. Over on the neighboring Grand Motte, Tignes has its own summer area, where it lives up to its boast of providing skiing 365 days a year.

Val d'Isère is on the edge of the Parc National de la Vanoise so there are marvellous opportunities for the keen photographer to spend afternoons below the snow line on camera safaris, getting pictures of marmottes, chamois and other wild animals as well as the beautiful flowers which clothe the slopes.

Kaprun, like Tignes, is a favorite area for the more serious summer skier, and training camps sponsored by clubs and ski manufacturers use its slopes. The camps are often led by famous names in the racing world – ex-champions who pass on their experience and inspiration to the next generation. Kaprun, in Austria, is in the mountainous Europa Sportregion of Salzburgerland. Transport is by three-stage cablecar, or by railway, which spurts from 3,400 ft to 9,170 ft, sometimes on stilts, sometimes through a tunnel, traveling so fast that it has to have its own decompression chamber at the top.

At the top is a mid-mountain complex which includes the Krefelder hut. This has 100 beds and acts as a hostel for many of the camps. From the midstation up to the Kitzsteinhorn there is a cablecar and with a chairlift and four tows there is plenty of space for summer skiing.

Kaprun has a gliding school and also indoor riding sheds for those who want to learn dressage. The Lippenzeller horses of Vienna are world famous and there is no shortage of dressage experts in Austria. There is also wonderful walking country to be explored off the Maiskogel mountain nearby.

Across the Atlantic, Bob Beattie runs a summer racing camp on Mount Bachelor in Oregon. Gymnastics start the day at 6.30 am and skiing can go on as late as 3.30 pm on the 10,000 ft volcanic mountain. Occasionally there is a day off for river-rafting, roller skating or horseback riding. At Whistler in British Columbia, Toni Sailer and Nancy Raine Green run weekly sessions for young racers. Squaw Valley in California specializes in race camps while Mount Hood, Arapahoe Basin, Mammoth Mountain and a dozen other resorts open up to skiers in June and July.

One of the great advantages of summer skiing all over the world is the variety of alternative sports to try out. When deciding where to go it is best to decide first which sport in addition to skiing is the most attractive and then pick the resort that has the best facilities.

Tennis is almost universal and, like skiing, it is often taught competitively by ex-champions. Some kind of swimming is always available, whether it is in the ice-cold waters of a mountain lake, in warm thermal springs bubbling up from far below the ground, or just in a swimming pool. Mountain walks are beautiful everywhere. Then there is a choice of sailing, rafting, wind-surfing and canoeing; golf, soccer, squash and volleyball. Fishing, yoga and karate are more

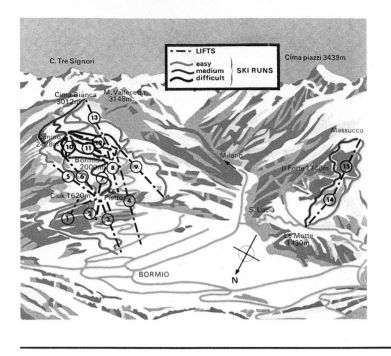

BORMIO
SKI FACTS
Top station 9,828 ft /
2 cable cars /
1 cabin /
2 chairs and 10 drags /
Maximum rise 3,290 ft /

specialised and mountaineering offers a great challenge.

Although the bleakness of winter disappears in summer, protection is still needed in the mountains. Early morning starts, lines on crowded slopes and cold chair lifts make a few layers of wool comfortable at the best of times. Gilets can be taken off as the sun gains strength but then again long sleeved cotton shirts help to protect untanned arms from too much sun. At altitude hats or eyeshades are getting very popular – both from fashionable and practical points of view. Suntan lotion is essential and, of course, dark-lensed sunglasses, for snow blindness is a very real danger. At altitude, energy is used up more quickly than oxygen can be breathed in, so those who are unfit tire quickly. Drinking lots of water and fruit juice helps to avoid dehydration.

All this sounds formidable but summer skiing provides the supreme adventure trip. Glorious weather, reliable snow conditions each morning and a great variety of occupations for the rest of the day turn the spindliest and most sun-starved town dweller into a healthy, strong, suntanned athlete after a couple of weeks of mountain air and exercise.

THE NON-SKIING PARTNER

Town and resort

maps
pages 89, 92

Innsbruck Nice Rome
Aosta Granada Sofia Oslo
Vancouver Grenoble

*S*kiing can bring dissension to a family. Often a husband skis but a wife does not or vice-versa. Sometimes the solution is simply for the skier to join a group of friends and leave the other behind but as couples want to introduce their children to skiing the pressure builds up on the non-skier to travel with them. The least the skier can do is find somewhere which is within reach of alternative entertainment, or go to a base, like New York or Helsinki, which has snow on its outskirts.

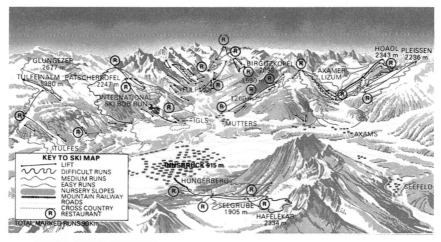

INNSBRUCK SKI FACTS
Top station 7,640 ft / 5 separate ski areas; Igls; Hungberburg;
Tulfes; Lizum; Mutters /
Glacier skiing on 10,000 ft Stubai Glacier /

Practically every well-equipped resort now has a heated pool, a skating rink and a cinema but the emphasis is still on skiing and the non-skier feels left out of the chat about the slopes in the evening. The solution is to find somewhere where a perfectly independent vacation can be had visiting museums, galleries, opera, theatre, and shops which do not sell only ski equipment.

An excellent European example is Innsbruck in Austria. The old city center has been closed to traffic and the painted houses lean across the streets as if to touch the wrought iron signs on the other side. The main thoroughfare is lined with exotic boutiques. Orchestras and theaters play nightly. It has as much to offer the winter visitor as it does to those who go there in summer. The only concession made by its many museums, art galleries and historic palaces is to open for slightly shorter hours and occasionally to remain closed on Sundays.

The old Gothic castle of the Hofburg was built first by Maximilian I and then rebuilt in rococco style by the Empress Maria Theresa in the 18th century. The empress also gave her name to the smartest shopping street of Innsbruck, which is crossed by a triumphal arch built in 1765. The Tirol museum contains a series of typical farmhouse interiors depicting life through the centuries including national costumes and field implements. The Tirol national museum has baroque paintings and statues as well as a good collection of old Dutch masters. The Cathedral of St Jakob is 18th century baroque.

While one member of the family is enjoying all this culture, the other can be taking advantage of the free bus service which the city of Innsbruck provides for skiers. From the center of the city buses go out each day to the many different ski resorts which encircle the city. Skiers can choose whether they want to ski crosscountry or downhill and the bus planning will insure that they are taken wherever the snow conditions are best.

Within an hour's drive all round, there are the most enchanting little valleys with crosscountry trails (they use the Norwegian word *loipe*) laid out alongside streams and through forests. Old inns provide good stopping places for lunch and the skier can decide just how far to go before turning back to be collected in the afternoon by the bus and brought back to Innsbruck.

For the ambitious, who want to pit themselves against the champions on an Olympic trail, Seefeld is one of the places to which the buses run and it has well signposted *loipe* of many standards. Seefeld also has good Alpine skiing on the Gschwandtkopf and Rosshütte mountains and is in a pocket where snow tends to lie even if it is scarce in other Austrian resorts.

Seefeld has a beautiful pool with a natural rock island round which an artificial current swirls, and a heated outdoor section where it is possible to swim comfortably while the snow is falling, and a big (mixed) sauna. The town is close to the German border and has its own smart, though expensive shops and restaurants, so it is a place which both skier and non-skier could visit together, ending the day perhaps with a visit to the casino.

Innsbruck has hosted the Olympics twice and the men's downhill run on the Patscherkofel is long and steep. The area at Axamer-Lizum, where the women's downhill takes place has some easier skiing. Mutters, Telfes and Neustift are all within reach for the day skier.

So the skier can fill each day happily skiing over new runs, while the non-skier is busy sightseeing. In the evening they can choose from Innsbruck's many restaurants. These range from medieval feasts in vaults where wild boar and mead are served to the accompaniment of a piper, to the elegant and historic Goldener Adler, near the riverside, and the Adambrau where clients sit at long tables and watch an excellent earthy folklore cabaret put on by the brewery.

Nice on the Côte d'Azur is another unlikely place for a skiing tour but Isola is only an hour-and-a-half up a winding road. Nice, like Innsbruck, has an old town with many fascinating restaurants, which specialize in Mediterranean fish dishes. The English first opened up Nice as an elegant and fashionable place to visit in winter and the Promenade des Anglais is imposing. Again, the casino makes a sophisticated alternative to the usual après-ski entertainment of accordion and disco found in small ski resorts.

Isola at 6,500 ft is confident enough of its skiing conditions to offer sun and snow guarantees through January, February and March and skiing usually goes on there into May. The resort first consisted only of one vast building, but it is now being developed with small chalets to soften the rather austere appearance. The skiing is not too difficult and the pistes are kept well flattened, so this is an excellent area for the beginner and it has long intermediate slopes, too.

Rome is a tourist city par excellence and there is no need to explain how a non-skier could fill weeks among its galleries and historic buildings. The skiing possibilities of Terminillo, however, are less well known. Yet this resort which is just an hour's drive from the Eternal City has lifts reaching up to 7,000 ft including a cablecar, a chairlift and many tows. This is not a resort for the expert, and snow here cannot be guaranteed but it can certainly provide a few days on the slopes for the tourist who hungers for snow.

Much more extensive skiing surrounds Pila, which can be reached direct from the ancient and exquisite little Roman town of Aosta. Aosta still has its medieval walls, an ancient abbey and the remains of its Roman amphitheater. Little old streets are full of life with shop owners chatting across at one another and selling ancient bric-a-brac and ski equipment side by side.

In Spain, Granada would make the most anti-skiing tourist sing with enthusiasm but just above, only 20 miles from the Alhambra is Solynieve which has an excellent snow record and good lift networks between 7,000 and 11,400 ft.

Sofia is a quite exotic destination for a tourist with its beautiful cathedral and city center. The Bulgarians keep the exchange rate for the lev at a very advantageous level for tourists and, as in many Eastern countries, there are special duty free shops for foreigners. Close to Sofia is Vitosha, a sunny and quite reliably snowy ski area with chairlifts and tows as well as good hire equipment.

Southern cities are not the only ones to attract tourists. Oslo in Norway has plenty to occupy the winter visitor. Just a short bus ride from the center are many crosscountry trails, lit as soon as darkness

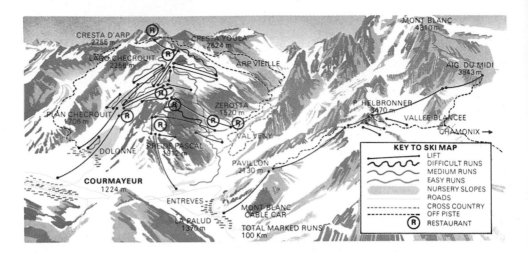

COURMAYEUR (AOSTA VALLEY) SKI FACTS
Top station 9,060 ft / 31 lifts including four-stage /
Cableway, largest cable car in the world. In Spring Mont Blanc cable car
runs to allow glacier skiing along Vallee Blanche down to
Chamonix on the French side /

---

falls, for the Norwegians are energetic people and enjoy their
evening's exercise after work.

Vancouver calls itself the world's largest ski village for it lies within
easy reach of Grouse, Hemlock and Whistler mountains. Grouse
mountain is only a quarter of an hour from the center of the city and the
big Superskyride cablecar goes straight up to 3,700 ft. There's a day
lodge up there, among the chairlifts and tows, with a big restaurant and
a disco for the evenings. All within sight of the city and the sea.

Grenoble, like Innsbruck a university town which has also hosted
the Olympics, is clustered with resorts. While the non-skier is visiting
the Musée des Beaux-Arts or the Eglise St-Laurent, the skier can be
enjoying Chamrousse, Villars de Lans, Alpe d'Huez and Les Deux
Alpes. Michelin has given a rosette and three knives and forks to
Poulards Bressane whose *Emince de volaille de Bresse* should be
enjoyed by all in the evening.

So there is no need for anyone to be a martyr to a skiing spouse.
Those who want to browse through museums can do so; orchestras
and opera are not always far from skislopes; even beaches for
sunbathing and waterskiing on the Mediterranean are within reach of
snow covered slopes.

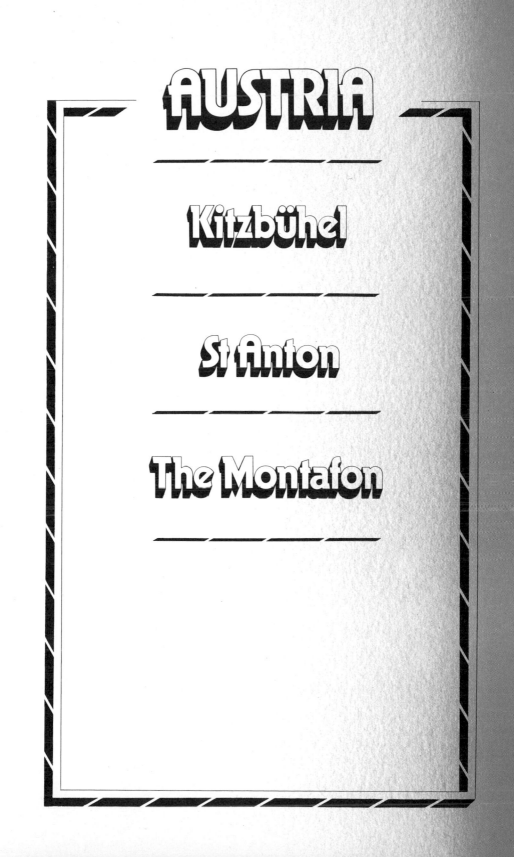

AUSTRIA

Kitzbühel

St Anton

The Montafon

AUSTRIA

Kitzbühel

map *page 96*

Kitzbühel is full of contrasts. Quite a large town, yet it feels like a medieval village; right in the heart of Austria, it attracts a cosmopolitan collection of skiers; best known for the steep swift drop of the Streif, it is surrounded by rolling Alpine pastures; its big hotels are palatial, yet the farmhouses in outlying villages offer simple and inexpensive bed and breakfast accommodation.

The history of skiing in Kitzbühel owes a great deal to one Norwegian. In 1890 the explorer Fridtjof Nansen published a book called *On Ski across Greenland*, explaining how helpful skis could be in reaching inaccessible territory. Franz Reisch, at that time mayor of Kitzbühel, read the book and wrote off to Norway to order a pair of skis. When they arrived at the local post office they were much admired and Franz Reisch set off to try them out. In spite of their length – 2.30 m (8 ft) he mastered them well enough to achieve a personal ambition and climb the Kitzbühelhorn. By 1893 he and his friends had formed the Kitzbühel Ski Association. Luckily one of Franz Reisch's great friends and collaborators was a photographer called Josef Herold, so the early exploits of the KSC are well documented. Early photographs show the ski pioneers in tweed jackets, with gaitered legs and single long poles which they used both for balance and for braking.

By 1900 visitors were coming to Kitzbühel to learn to ski and to try out different techniques. Colonel Bilgeri brought troops to train there for mountain warfare, W. R. Rickmers was an early technician and ran a school.

Kitzbühel built up its reputation as a race resort very early on. In the 'thirties Kitzbühel opened up to visitors from all over the world. They still pour in, now from Sweden, Holland, America, Germany, Britain, Italy and Spain. It remains a very cosmopolitan resort.

The old walled town center has recently been closed entirely to traffic. The gabled houses, crowd together, painted bright, even clashing colors. It is a tempting place to wander, looking at the old

Location
The medieval village lies in its surrounding Austrian Kitzbüheler Alpen between Innsbruck to the South West and Salzburg to the North. It became a ski resort before the end of the 19th century.

Ski areas
Hahnenkamm, Kitzbüheler Horn (6,450 ft), Bichelalm, Jochberg-Pass Thurn; 75 miles of linked pistes between 2,500 ft and 6,500 ft high. A resort to suit all skiers, with 53 lifts, including 4 cablecars and 12 chairs.

Accommodation
A wide range of large and small, traditional and newer hotels, plus *pensions*.

Activities
Fitness rooms, swimming pools, a whirlpool, saunas, solariums, gambling, afternoon tea and tea dancing, and folklore evenings.

shops, stopping for hot chocolate and whipped cream with delicious *Apfelstrudel* or rich creamy cakes.

The joy and pride of Kitzbühel is its ski circus, for it was one of the first resorts at which skiers could travel across the mountains from one lift to another, rather than up and down a particular area. So Kirchberg, Aurach, Jochberg, Aschau and Pass Thurn all developed, first into places that Kitzbühel visitors skied down to, and then into small resorts in their own right. They link through Kitzbühel's four main ski areas: the Hahnenkamm, the Kitzbüheler Horn, Bichelalm and Jochberg, Pass Thurn; with lifts from Kirchberg also going up to Gaisberg.

A good deal of emphasis is given to taking advantage of all the long trails. There is a special run, marked with elephant symbols and called Ski-safari Kitzbühel, which takes the good skier 22 miles across country from Kitzbühel to Pass Thurn. The ski school also organizes overnight tours.

The Hahnenkamm cableway rises straight from the town center at 2,600 ft to 5,400 ft – or there is a two-stage chair lift. From here no less than 8 chair lifts and 6 ski lifts interconnect to cover Ehrenbachhohe, the Steinbergkogel and Pengelstein, the highest point at 6,380 ft. The Kitzbüheler Horn at 6,450 ft is reached from a cablecar just across the other side of the resort. There is a mid-station with a wide sunny bowl used as a nursery and a big area of pistes and off piste slopes to be enjoyed by intermediates.

Bichelalm has a long chair lift rising from Aurach and from the top are two tows covering Hochetz and Stuchkogel. Again, this is a good area for off piste skiing with a long ridge off which many runs lead to Oberaurach or Fieberbrunn. On the way from Kitzbühel towards Mittersill, the road crosses Pass Thurn, where the skiing is high enough to last until late Spring. The skibus – included on the liftpass – is invaluable to ski tourers, covering most of the villages except Fieberbrunn and St Johann.

The whole circus of 60 lifts covers 75 miles of pistes between 2,500 ft and 6,500 ft. Used for centuries as cow pastures they are pleasantly rounded and covered with grass. The fun is to travel across them, choosing steep or easy pistes as the feeling goes, coming down to small villages, stopping for a coffee or lunch at an old valley inn; back up the lift and home across the mountains again. This is the contrast to setting off down the Streif, heart in mouth, to emulate the great racers.

Kitzbühel houses a big skiing population, so inevitably queues build up for the cablecars in the mornings. The town does its best to reduce them by providing a shuttle bus to siphon off those who might wait to lifts that are not crowded.

One of the most famous racers of all time, Toni Sailer, who won all three gold medals (downhill, slalom and giant slalom) at the 1956 Olympic Games still lives in Kitzbühel and runs the very big ski school there. The instructors are known as the Red Devils but betray their name by running an excellent children's ski school. Like most Kitzbühelers, they nearly all speak excellent English.

If any resort suits all skiers it is Kitzbühel. The big ski school has a well practised technique for beginners and wide, easy slopes on which they can learn. There is a huge area of fairly easy Alps, for daily

KITZBUHEL SKI FACTS
Top station 6,400 ft / 4 cable cars / 12 chairs /
10 drags / Maximum rise 2,943 ft /

---

excursions either on or off the piste. Expert skiers right up to world class racers, are extended on the steep slopes of the Streif. Kitzbühel is relatively low but its central position in the European landmass preserves the snow from mid-December to mid-March and up on Pass Thurn the lifts stay open into April.

The hotels at Kitzbühel have developed over the centuries with all the variety one would expect of an old town. The Tiefenbrunner, lying just inside the ancient gateway, was recently brought up to date with swimming pool, sauna and solarium. The big old bedrooms were restructured to include bathrooms and, so that no one is disturbed by noise, the children have a special playroom of their own. The comfortable bar, with a door out onto the pavement, is still the traditional place to talk over the day's skiing. The buffet breakfasts in the restaurant have only one drawback – it is easy to eat too much.

The Weisses Rossl (white horse) is also in the old part of town and has recently been rebuilt into a modern luxury hotel. At the Goldene Greif there is a casino where gamblers can try roulette, Black Jack or Baccara. For those who prefer more modest surroundings, there are fifty or sixty small *pensions* offering bed and breakfast. Kitzbühel caters for the sporting. The big hotels have fitness rooms and even some of the smallest offer table tennis.

The Kitzbühel pool and sauna complex is excellent. It houses two pools, a whirlpool, solarium, sauna, bars, restaurants and underwater massage. All this is free on the liftpass.

After a day on the slopes, Praxmair's is the place for tea and Seppi's for later in the evening. There are good discos at the Tenne, the Drop In and King's Club. Kitzbühel is not Tyrolean for nothing; it has folklore evenings and tea dancing still goes on as it did in the time of King Edward VIII. Fondues and fashion evenings all give plenty to do after skiing.

St Anton

map
page 100

It is difficult to get away from history at St Anton. Because it lies on a high pass along the main route between central Switzerland and Vienna, it was one of the very first ski resorts. As far back as 1907 Hannes Schneider, who was to have such an influence on its development, was already giving ski lessons there. By 1922 he had founded the famous Arlberg School.

St Anton, Austria

Hannes Schneider did not like the sweeping Telemark turns invented by the Norwegians to control speed – he complained they pinched his toes. Instead, he persuaded his pupils to point their ski tips together and press their heels apart. This snow plough effect helped them to stop quickly and with control came the confidence to increase speed. Early racers learned to lean far forward over the tips of their skis in what became known as the Arlberg crouch. Teaching technique continued to develop with counter-rotation, a distinctive twist between shoulders, hips and knees. For a long while the Arlberg School led the way in technique. Thousands still flock to learn from its instructors who now work under the direction of the ex-World Champion racer Karl Schranz.

Each morning skiers new to St Anton crowd onto the ski school meeting place to be sorted swiftly into classes according to their ability, their fitness and the language they understand. With 300 instructors, no learner needs suffer the misery of being far worse, or the boredom of being far better than the others in the class.

Learning is a serious business in St Anton, leavened only by the Austrian sense of humor which breaks through as a class collapses into tumbled heaps over a practise slope. Somehow the young instructors never lose their sense of the ridiculous however cold they may get waiting about on the slopes. 'We are not making a cemetary', calls the young man, as he encourages his class to their feet to try again.

Beginners need to be young and fit, as they climb up small inclines to traverse and turn their way down again for the two hours between ten and twelve each morning. After lunch they are rewarded by free skiing between two and four. Following in the tracks of their teacher, they explore the slopes, using lifts and trying out all the lessons they learnt so painfully in the morning.

It is not only the beginner who goes to ski school in St Anton, for the top classes go right up to racing standard. No one is ashamed to be seen learning from a navy-clad St Anton instructor. Before Christmas special courses are held to prepare serious skiers for the season ahead of them. The short steep slopes make perfect practise terrain for tight turns. They also make good race courses. History was made again in St Anton when British ski pioneer Arnold Lunn came to visit Hannes Schneider and in 1928 they founded the Arlberg-Kandahar Race. The first downhill, slalom and combined event took place then and, now alternating between Garmisch, Chamonix and St Anton, the Arlberg-Kandahar is still one of the top half-dozen races on the World Cup circuit.

Three of St Anton's four main lifts start from the West end of the village across the railway line which forms its northern boundary. The Galzigbahn goes to the top of a sugar loaf mountain, flattish on top, steeper at the sides, with runs back to St Anton or over the other side to the neighbouring village of St Christoph. Another lift up to Gampen and Kapall (7,631 ft) gives access to several intermediate runs and to the steep Kandahar face. The biggest lift is the cablecar which leaps across two valleys and deposits skiers right up the Valluga at 9,222 ft. From here there are spectacular panoramas across to the Lechtal Alps to the North, and across the Verwall and the Silvretta to the South.

Extra lifts were recently erected in this area up the Schindlergrat to the Ulmerhütte and the Valfagehrbahn to the Valluga. Big steep runs lead back to St Anton.

Long lines still build up for the Valluga and Galzig lifts, although the fourth ski area on the Rendl has helped to release the pressure out of the village. This long-awaited development goes up to Gampberg at 7,874 ft and opens up much-needed North and North West facing slopes which skiers find particularly pleasant, as they catch the afternoon sunshine.

Beginners use the short Nasserein tow at the eastern end of the village which serves some gentle slopes. Expert skiers who live in this part of St Anton use the tow, too, as a useful hitch across to the start of the Valluga, Galzig and Kapall lifts.

From 1980 the St Anton lift pass has been linked with the lift passes of Zurs and Lech over the Flexen Pass, as well with those of the nearby villages of St Christoph and Stuben. All this gives the skier some 67 lifts to choose from. Buses run regularly between the five villages, though there is no piste beaten between St Anton and the Lech-Zurs area. Zurs is compact, pretty and sophisticated. Lech, with Ober-Lech above it, is more spread out and suits families well. Both share an excellent ski area, which is well worth the expedition from St Anton. St Christoph, directly connected via the Kapall area has short, easy slopes and Stuben benefits from the steep, north facing Albona mountain.

At one time the traffic which flowed along the main pass road through St Anton threatened to turn St Anton into a traffic nightmare, where it clashed with the skiers' cars which choked the narrow streets. A bypass now takes care of the through traffic and visitors' cars are firmly directed by the police to big car parks. A pedestrian precinct makes a little haven which has brought back the village atmosphere. The onion domed church and old painted hotels make it unmistakeably Tyrolean, while the well dressed crowd which throngs the streets comes from all over the world.

Australians have a special fondness for this part of Austria and in St Anton they have their own bar, the Krazy Kangaroo which they run with some Swedes.

FACTS

Location
Village on the high pass between central Switzerland and Innsbruck, just East of Liechtenstein. The Arlberg Pass has given its name to St Anton's famous ski school.

Ski areas
Gampen and Kapall (7,631 ft), Rendl, the Kandahar, Ulmer-hütte, Valluga (9,222 ft). Close by is the Lech-Zurs resort and the village of St Christophe. The entire area is served by nearly 70 lifts.

Accommodation
Several hotels and a wide variety of *pensions*; social life in the bars and tea shops.

Activities
St Anton, home of the Arlberg School, places the emphasis almost entirely on skiing. It is also a summer ski resort. There are saunas, skating, billiards and bowling.

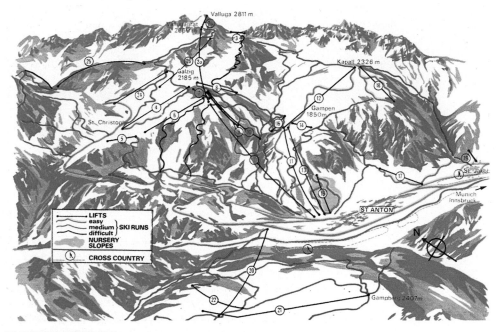

ST ANTON SKI FACTS
Top station 9,192 ft / 1 funicular / 4 cable cars /
1 cabin / 2 chairs and 18 drags / Maximum rise 2,515 ft /

Meaty paprika goulasch soup in one of the quick-service mountain restaurants gives just the energy needed to spend the afternoon skiing hard over challenging slopes. Then it is time to come down to hot chocolate and *Apfelstrudel* covered with whipped cream. A stroll round the shops perhaps and then into the warm hubbub of the Rosannastuberl where so many English-speaking travelers congregate in the evening. A last drink in one of the many bars and it is time for bed to prepare for another strenuous day.

Still among the most luxurious hotels is the old coaching house The Post, which continues the tradition of tea-dancing. There are about twenty hotels in the village and as many as a couple of hundred houses which offer scrupulously clean, warm, simple rooms with breakfast at very reasonable prices.

St Anton is ideal for the serious skier who wants to improve his already strong technique in a top resort without spending too much. It is possible to stay cheaply and without distraction at a simple *pension*. On a typical day, after an early start to beat the rush hour, the morning is spent working hard in class on stance, weight transference, balance and attack.

The Montafon

Gargellen   Schruns
Gaschurn   Brand

maps
*pages 101,
104*

There is nothing like the atmosphere of an old
Austrian village to give color to a vacation. Old brown chalets
clustered round a church with a bulbous-belfry; dark wooden walls
and a thick coating of snow on the roof; steep pathways winding up
between cow byres; Christmas trees by the door and chamois on the
slopes. It is the picture postcard ideal of a ski resort.

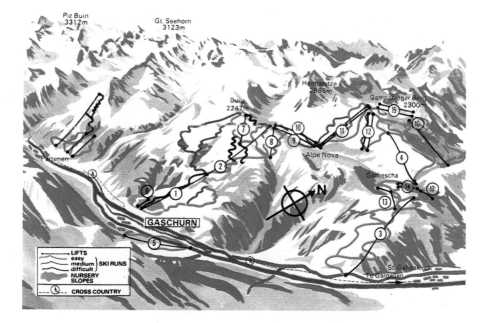

GASCHURN SKI FACTS
Top station 7,521 ft / 6 chairs /
11 drags / Maximum rise 2,119 ft /

One such village is Gargellen, in the Montafon Valley, a valley which contains several resorts and ski areas. Drivers coming from Switzerland into Austria turn right at the busy border town of Bludenz, and continue into a broad, sunny, well populated valley. In summer the rural scene is of fruit-trees below and Jersey-colored cows on the grassy Alpine slopes above, but in winter the snow is reliable from Christmas until the end of March, even though most of the villages are low.

The road was first metalled for a huge hydroelectric scheme and there are several dams with generating stations in the mountains. In summer it is possible to continue on over the Silvretta road to the Paznauntal where Ischgl has developed its own snow circus with Samnaun in Switzerland but the high point on the road at Bielerhohe is over 7,000 ft and closes in winter.

Gargellen lies due South of St Gallenkirch which is right in the middle of the Montafon valley. It is the answer to a beginner's prayer. Small and compact, it has only ten hotels and its onion-domed church might have come straight out of a picture book. As the nursery slopes run right into the village, there is no awkward tramping in unfamiliar ski boots in the morning and no trudging back, tired at the end of the day. Parents can sit in the comfortable old Madrisa Hotel and watch their children playing safely on the slopes. Zithers and *Schuhenplattler* dancing enliven the candlelit evenings. No traffic passes through the village as it lies at the top of the valley. At 4,672 ft, with lifts up to the Schafberg mountain at 7,546 ft, the slopes are snow-sure. Perhaps the only problem is that Gargellen is both perfect and popular, and the hotels are booked up from year to year. It is not only a beginner's paradise – the slopes challenge even the expert. The Montafon valley lies in the spectacular Silvretta region, long known to ski-tourers, which stretches over the border. From Gargellen there is a route down to Klosters in Switzerland.

The Montafon valley contains two other well-known areas for intermediate skiers. Schruns, the capital, has a thriving market town. Those of its people not caught up with tourism, manufacture *Loden*, the thick felted cloth often a distinctive dark green which keeps off the wind and rain. Schruns is also a spa and the mineral water is used in a health hydro. The Hotel Lowe in its center channels the spa water into a beautiful swimming pool. Although quite big and on the main road, Schruns has managed to keep its old buildings. Ernest Hemingway discovered Schruns in the 1920s, which he described as 'a sunny market town with sawmills, stores, inns and a good year-round hotel called the Taube, where we stayed'.

The skiing is quite testing; indeed Schruns has long been the venue for a major ladies race which alternates yearly with one at Bad Gastein. The top lifts to the Senniggrat and Kreuzjoch cover rather daunting slopes but the areas between Kappall, the middle station of the cablecar, and the double Seebliga lifts are easily mastered, and there are gently graded runs down to the valley floor.

Further South up the valley, past the turning off for Gargellen, lies the relatively new area of Silvretta Nova. Here the building of the Gampabinger lift has linked the skiing from Garfrescha with the

Versettla slopes above Gaschurn. A cablecar, five chairs and twenty-five tows can lift thirty thousand skiers an hour. As there are only 3,000 guest beds in the villages below, the lift capacity copes easily with the number of skiers and no queues form. A great deal of skiing can be done over the 40 miles of runs between 6,600 ft and 3,300 ft in a short time, the only temptation to linger coming from the superb sight of the mountain ranges stretching away into the distance.

The Montafon is not the only valley which provides good skiing in the region. Also reached from Bludenz is the Brandnertal which leads up to the great dammed lake of Lunersee.

The road winds along with beautiful views of the Scesaplana mountain which forms the barrier between Austria and Switzerland. Within a few miles from Bludenz lies Burserberg with a small network of lifts and then, ten minutes further on is Brand, another excellent area for beginners. Its old dark chalets show the influence of the refugees from the Valais area of Switzerland, who came here to escape religious persecution in the 13th and 14th centuries.

There are plenty of modern hotels in Brand, which has more than 2,000 tourist beds. There is an excellent ski school and a nursery slope which is wide and gentle right by the village. A kindergarden looks after 3 to 8-year olds right through the day and by the age of four children can join the ski school.

At each end of the village is a chair lift and they link on the slopes above to cover a good area between 3,434 ft and 6,290 ft. The lift pass can also be used at Bürserberg.

So the Montafon and Brand offer an easy answer to the difficult question of where families might start skiing. Convenient nursery slopes and good ski schools are complemented by extensive slopes for the better skiers in the family.

FACTS

Location
The Montafon valley is almost on the Austrian-Swiss border, just South of St Anton and over the border from Klosters. The valley lies in the Silvretta region and contains several resorts and ski areas.

Ski villages
St Gallenkirch, Gargellen, Schruns, the new Silvretta Nova area; and close to the Montafon Valley, the Brandnertal region. The well-tended runs cater for all standards. There are over 50 lifts.

Accommodation
Montafon is scattered with little hotels; over 2,000 beds in the town of Brand. Good social life in the hotels.

Activities
Schruns is a spa town and has a health hydro. Otherwise, the area concentrates on skiing and is well suited to families and beginners.

following page
Shruns, Brand, maps ▶

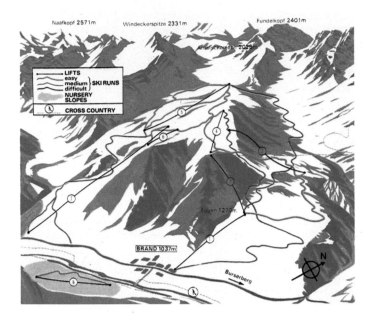

BRAND
SKI FACTS
Top station 6,608 ft /
3 chairs /
5 drags /
Maximum rise 1,825 ft /

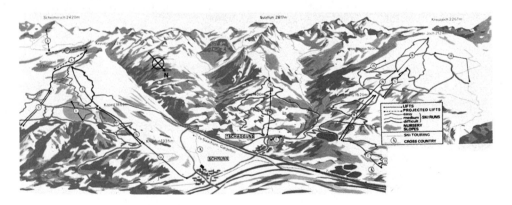

SCHRUNS
SKI FACTS
Top station
7,397 ft /
2 funiculars /
2 cable cars /
7 chairs and 10 drags /
Maximum rise
3,760 ft /

Taking the kids

There was a time when couples had to give up skiing when they started families, because it was difficult to find baby minders in the mountains and ski schools did not want to cope with children who were not old enough to know how to keep themselves warm and dry in the snow. Now all that has changed. Practically every resort provides special facilities and care for young children and parents find that a skiing holiday gives them a rare chance to have a real change, skiing by day and eating out in the evening while their children are well cared for.

There is one resort in particular – Flaine in the French Alps just 40 minutes drive from Geneva airport – which specializes in looking after children. Ever since it was first planned by Eric Boissonas, and opened in 1971, Flaine has had families in mind. The Hotel les Lindars, set right in the center, would have solved all the problems of the old woman who lived in a shoe. Infants have their own day *creche* in Les Lindars,

Learning the easy way

where they are free to lie in cots or roll around in play pens. Specially qualified nannies give them their bottles, change and generally care for them from 9 am to 6 pm.

Once past infancy, the children graduate to the *jardin des enfants*, which also accepts children from outside the hotel. It consists of a big airy day nursery, well equipped with toys and child-size furniture. As the children come in the door, snowy hats, jackets and boots are whipped off and deposited on a row of tiny hooks and lockers. The children settle to finger painting, castle building or other games in groups according to age. The groups go out in turn for walks, to play in the snow or, as soon as they are old enough, to learn to ski. Lunch and tea are supervised round small tables. Outside in the snow nursery there are snowmen to make, cartoon characters to play around and a carousel with long arms to hold onto, just to get the feel of skis moving underfoot as the arms slowly revolve.

Ski lessons start for children as young as three years old. Flaine has a wide sunny nursery area just to the side of the main square. It is well pisted and there is an easy tow and slow-running chair so that children can learn to use them confidently. From 6 pm when the *jardin* closes until 10 pm the Hotel les Lindars runs a children's club with supervised games and a library to keep them happy during the later part of the evening.

Bedrooms in the hotel are equipped with microphones, which can be switched on between 7 pm and midnight when children are left asleep. At a central consol a couple of girls listen. If there are cries from one of the intercoms, one of the girls goes off to make sure that everything necessary is done to make the child comfortable and content again. Parents leave their telephone numbers so they can be contacted if there is a crisis, and they can then go out with a clear conscience.

Other resorts have learned from Flaine's success in attracting young families. In Avoriaz, not far off, the children's village is run by two ex-racers, Isabel Mir and Annie Famose, so it is perhaps not surprising that the competitive spirit is encouraged with fun and competitions. In these races, everyone seems to win and youngsters return home proudly wearing their badges.

For those who do not want to stay at a hotel, condominiums and self-catering flats offer a good home background for children, where they can keep what hours suit them, have the food they are accustomed to eat and make a noise without disturbing the people in the next room. Northstar at Tahoe is excellent for young families, for its condominiums are set in the quiet of the California pines. The layout of the lifts in the ski area is simple and all runs channel back to the village so there is no problem about getting lost. Children from 6 to 12 years old can be left with the ski school from 10 am to 4 pm.

Vail, in Colorado, is an example of a big ski area which does not forget the small skier. The child who gave the name to the Lost Boy trail was found long before he suffered any lasting harm. There are special areas for children including Peanut Peak near the popular Eagles Nest Lionshead lift top. A nursery takes care of children from two to six and ski school operates at two points for six to twelve year olds between 9.30 am and 3.30 pm daily.

Children's ski clothes are now warm and waterproof enough to keep them comfortable even when out in blizzards. Hats that fit snugly over ears and tie round chins, suits that zip up to keep out draughts, fleece-lined boots and gloves on strings that slot through armholes, all contribute to comfort and safety.

Many schools, both in North America and in Europe, appreciate that a skiing vacation can also be an educational experience and send classes away to the mountains for a couple of weeks even in term-time. Teachers become ski party leaders, though most are content to leave the actual business of ski teaching to mountain-based instructors. Many tour operators specialise in school parties. They generally offer resorts which have fairly limited facilities and hostel-type accommodation. Good equipment hire and good instruction are more important than luxurious bedrooms and exciting night clubs. Bulgarians and northern Italians are particularly patient with children. Their resorts are inexpensive and are popular among schools.

Fast skiers who show promise by the age of 10 are well advised to contact racing clubs which organize junior training without delay. Many people do not realise that the racer seen speeding down a world cup course has probably trained every holiday for as long as ten years before attaining that seemingly effortless speed. It is too late to decide to become a racer at 16.

Junior training is no picnic. The qualities which go to make a good racer – energy, determination and competitive spirit – are often those which lead to liveliness off the slopes too. Junior training managers require as much stamina as their charges. Resorts with short steep slopes and a compact village where errant trainees can be swiftly located such as Mürren (Switzerland) or Alpbach (Austria) make good junior training areas. The would-be racers are adjured to arrive fit at the beginning of their stay in the mountains, and the days are spent in exercise, training through slalom poles and perfecting technique.

The Alpine and eastern-block countries have special schools for prospective racers where classrooms and mountain slopes are both used for lessons. One which has provided many champions is at Schladming in the Austrian region of Styria.

Many equipment manufacturers run training camps for promising youngsters, offering special rates in return for loyalty to their products. At Kaprun, near Kitzbuhel, there is a big hostel on the Kitzsteinhorn which operates throughout the summer for junior race trainees. They ski early in the morning on the great glacial slopes, swim in the warm afternoons and do fitness training in the evenings.

Childhood is the time to learn to ski, whether it is as a holiday sport or for a racing career. Children seem to suffer less fear of falling, of height or of being made to feel ridiculous. Without bothering too much with technique they manage to learn by imitating their instructors. The only problems parents have when they bring their children with them on holiday is how to explain why they themselves get left so quickly behind.

following page
Flaine, Ávoriaz, maps ▶

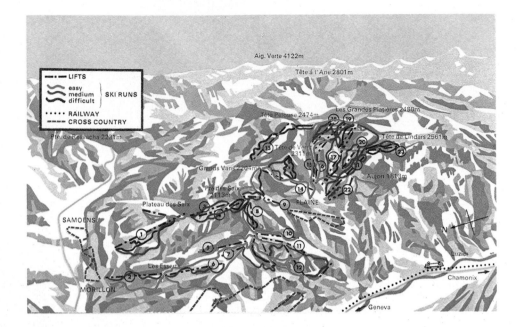

FLAINE SKI FACTS
Top station 8,197 ft / 1 cable car / 3 cabins /
10 chairs and 9 drags / Maximum rise 3,165 ft /

AVORIAZ SKI FACTS
Top station 8,928 ft / 1 cable car / 5 cabins /
20 chairs and 60 drags / Maximum rise 3,641 ft /

WORLD-WIDE SKIING

Scotland

Finland

Australia

New Zealand

South America

Scotland

Cairngorm   Glenshee
Glencoe   The Lecht

maps
pages
112–113

Perhaps the most predictable thing about the weather on Cairngorm is that it is unpredictable. Standing outside the Ptarmigan restaurant at 3,600 ft it is possible to look out over Strathspey and watch the bands of cloud approaching, interspersed with clear sky. Within minutes the weather changes from clear to blizzard, from rain to clear again.

Wind is the predominant factor and occasionally it even brings the lifts to a halt. But the Scots are hardy and use the wind to build their pistes. Because it frequently blows horizontally across The Highlands, carrying the snow with it, snow fences are erected along the sides of the pistes to trap the snow where it is needed. This, and the fact that the moors are deeply etched with stream beds which fill in winter with many feet of snow, keeps well-packed ribbons of snow snaking down the mountainside. Even when the wind carries in salty rain from the sea to melt the cover from the surrounding hillsides, the ribbons remain.

The best time to ski in Scotland is usually March to May, when anti cyclones often bring clear skies for days at a time. The quality of snow is often heavy, for the water content is high, but it packs well down and is less likely to avalanche than Alpine powder.

Cairngorm, ninety miles north of Perth, is the most developed of Scotland's four ski areas. The chair lifts up two adjoining gullies (called *coires* in Scotland) meet on the Ptarmigan plateau. Another gulley, Lurchers, is projected but development here has been long delayed by conservationists.

The Cairngorm chair lift from the main car park at 2,000 ft goes up to a mid station, where the Sheiling restaurant makes a useful meeting place and center of activity for the many races which are held on Cairngorm. From this level rise a tow and chairlift serving the White Lady trail, a ski tow which is used primarily by racers on the M1 course, and the Coire Cas tow. Over to the right rises the Fiacaill tow and the gentle slopes run down from it right to the car park. Joining this network is the Coire na Ciste series of chair lifts and tows coming up from another car park at 1,800 ft.

The slopes are heavily used, especially when the weather is good. Eager skiers pour in from the surrounding villages, arrive by train on the main Edinburgh to Aviemore railway line and come by the coachload from the cities of Northern England. Queues build up at the lifts and skiers learn to slalom down crowded slopes.

Should the weather deteriorate and the winding 9-mile road get blocked, there is plenty to do apart from skiing in what has become Scotland's best developed vacation area. The Aviemore Center has accommodation to suit everyone, from the luxurious Strathspey Hotel to self-catering chalets and cheap hotels. There are excellent shops, a big swimming pool, squash courts and two artificial slopes for those who feel they must ski even if not on snow. Both ice skating and that great Scottish pastime, curling, are provided for in a big indoor rink. There are saunas, solarium, dancing, discos, a cinema and a theatre, and children are specially catered for in Santa Claus Land, which includes a miniature train as well as an exhibition of British Kings and Queens. Those in search of an ancestry can look up their surnames on a register and find out which clan is associated with them – and there is a tartan to go with every clan.

The Center is a summer resort too, for fishermen, stalkers, pony trekkers, mountaineers, bird watchers and those who just enjoy walking in The Highlands.

At least a dozen villages within easy reach of Cairngorm offer accommodation in comfortable pubs, and bed and breakfast in local homes. Hospitality is warm in these solid, stonebuilt farmhouses. Good drying rooms take care of the Scottish mist; hotwater bottles warm the beds and every morning breakfasts of porridge, kippers, sausages and oatcakes send off the skiers well sustained for the day. A bus works slowly round the various villages and drops skiers up at the Cairngorm car park.

Several ski schools were established on these slopes in the 1950's and 1960's with instructors mainly from Austria and Norway. Gradually the Scots have been taking over, coordinating the best ideas from each national school, and they now form a well skilled team with a distinctive style. They attend the ski teachers' biennial Interski Meeting, and contribute practical ideas of their own.

There is plenty of wild life in the Highlands. In winter the herds of red deer come down to feed below the snow line. Reindeer had died out but a small herd was reintroduced from Lapland in 1952 and the numbers are growing. Ptarmigan is quite common, the pigeon-sized bird of the grouse family, and late in the spring the rare osprey flies in to nest near Loch Garten.

Glenshee is the next biggest ski area in Scotland and it lies South East of Aviemore on the Perth-Braemar road. The chair lift up Cairnwell mountain runs from 2,000 ft to over 3,000 ft and there are four major tows to support it. On the other side of the road a similar system serves the South facing slopes of Meal Odhar.

The Fife Arms at Braemar is a luxury hotel only miles from the slopes and the Log Cabin Hotel at Kirkmichael, traditionally built with a turf

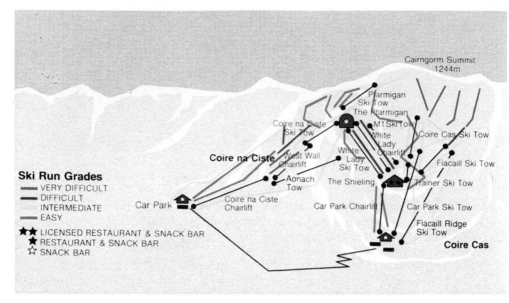

CAIRNGORM

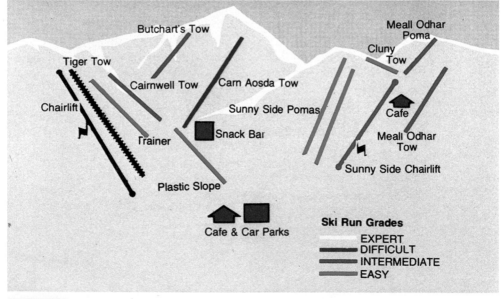

GLENSHEE

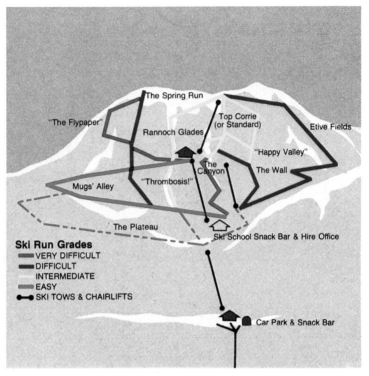

Ski Run Grades
- VERY DIFFICULT
- DIFFICULT
- INTERMEDIATE
- EASY
- SKI TOWS & CHAIRLIFTS

GLENCOE

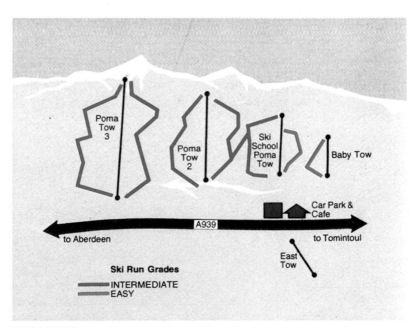

Ski Run Grades
- INTERMEDIATE
- EASY

THE LECHT

roof, shows ski films while skiers sip *Glühwein* round a log fire. These hotels also provide a full supporting schedule. An increasingly popular event is the Sno Fun week in March, when the locals turn up in fancy dress, there are competitions to see how many people can ski on one pair of skis and Toss-the-wellie tests everyone's boot throwing skill. The days end with Scotland's version of a wild musical party, the Ceilidh.

The third area, Glencoe, operates only at weekends and over the New Year and Easter weeks. It can, however, be opened for clubs who hire the lift and take over the mountainside for themselves during the week. The setting is wild and beautiful, rising out of Rannoch Moor and known for the memory of the Glencoe Massacre when Macdonalds were treacherously murdered by Campbells in 1762. Access is quite easy for the base is low and the first chair lift is built mainly to bring skiers up to the snow line. The slope above, covered by a second chair and two tows gives a vertical drop of 1,300 ft and is considered by most skiers as the best ski slope in the country.

Finally a small area has recently been opened at The Lecht, on the road by Tomintoul, the highest village in Britain. This gently graded bowl holds the snow when it is scarce elsewhere and provides easy slopes. Families come so that parents can get some exercise and keep their children within sight as they become accustomed to their skis.

Scotland may have problems in unpredictable weather and slopes that get crowded when conditions are good but it can provide excellent skiing and a very warm welcome. Families never get bored as they try out all the different sports and occupations provided. There is also the excellent spirit of The Highlands to sustain parents. Distilleries have been built where the soft water gives whisky its finest flavor. After a day battling with wind and snow, ranging over the wild moorland, there comes the time to sit by a peat and wood fire with a glass of malt whisky to warm the heart.

FACTS

Location
The Cairngorm range, which reaches 4,084 ft at the highest place, is served by the village of Aviemore, 90 miles North of Perth. Glenshee lies South East of Aviemore on the Perth-Braemar road. Glencoe rises out of Rannoch Moor to the East of Scotland. The Lecht is North East of The Cairngorms, on the road by Tomintoul in Banff.

Aviemore's Coire Cas has 2 chair lifts and 7 tows; nearby Coire na Ciste has 2 chair lifts, 3 tows and a poma. Glenshee is served by nearly 10 lifts. White Corries, Glencoe, essentially a weekend resort, has one chair Lecht, principally for families and beginners, has 5 lifts.

Ski areas
The Cairngorms, Glenshee, Glencoe and The Lecht.

Accommodation
Aviemore has hotels, self-catering chalets, pubs, and bed and breakfast homes, a pattern shared but on a decreasing scale, especially in the small resorts of Glencoe and The Lecht.

Activities
Aviemore has two artificial slopes, ice skating, curling, saunas, solarium, dancing, discos and a cinema; there are also red deer, reindeer and a large variety of birds. The Glenshee hotels provide a full social and sporting schedule. Families are welcomed at all the Scottish resorts.

WORLD-WIDE SKIING

Finland

About a fifth of Finland's surface area is covered by lakes, and in winter the ice freezes several feet thick. The earliest snow comes to the far North of Finland, Lapland, as early as September or October, lasting until early April in the South and until even June in the North. The Finns ski as others might jog. Illuminated ski tracks cover the outskirts of Helsinki for local keep-fit enthusiasts, and slalom slopes have been cleared and ski lifts constructed all over the country since the 1960s.

Ski treks 30 to 125 miles long are arranged at the weekends outside Helsinki. Arranged guided tours make trips into the Lapland wilderness of about 50 to 100 miles, generally in March and April, when the afternoon sun softens the snowcrust and the night frost freezes it over with a thin layer of ice. This is the country, together with like facilities and attitudes in Sweden, Norway and all over Lapland, for an unsophisticated, hard, happy ski break with the local people, unequalled anywhere else.

Houses are well spread out in the villages, and people have adapted their lives so completely to the snow that if a housewife lives in an isolated spot on the shores of a lake, she simply skis across it in winter to do the shopping. It is quicker and easier than going round. Anyone wanting to learn crosscountry skiing will find that the lakes in Finland have beautifully flat surfaces. However, the Forest Lake Hotel ski school and practise tracks that lies between Helsinki and its airport, gives fair skiing for those who have business in the capital and a couple of days to spare.

The seasons around the Arctic Circle where many of the ski centers cluster, vary intensely with the hours of daylight. Winter brings the deep twilight the Finns call *kaamos*, when the sun scarcely rises, but spring is the best time for a skiing vacation. By April there are twelve hours of daylight over most of the country and this includes plenty of clear sunshine. The areas are so vast between ski resorts that it is

easiest to fly to them from Helsinki. Looking down from the aircraft, all that can be seen is mile upon mile of forest and lake.

Kilpisjärvi in the far North West corner of the country, well above the Arctic Circle, has a varied ski program. A ski week there includes all-day trips, with lunchtime picnics eaten round a fire. Lunch can even be fished straight out of a lake with a rod and line through a hole cut in the ice. There are treks along prepared trails, covering about 20 miles a day, or much longer ones out in the wilderness with a guide, for the really fit and experienced trekker.

Around the Arctic Circle are several small villages, with often just one hotel, within easy reach of Rovaniemi, and characterized by hills or fells on which it is possible to ski downhill. The Finns call it slalom skiing. Hotel Revontuli on Sella Fell has a fine view across Russia. Most of the facilities are basic, but Kultakero hotel does have a chair lift up Pyhatunturi fell.

The Hotel Suommu at Suomutunturi has a double tow. It also has a striking restaurant built like a huge Lapp tent; at night the pole star gleams down the smoke hole at the top. As well as having its slalom hill, Suomutunturi is a good center for crosscountry, with 45 miles of varied, well-marked trails through sparse forests. A comfortable 5-mile ski from the hotel leads to Lehtoniemi farmhouse lying beside a frozen lake. It has a particularly good sauna where skiers can sit and sweat away the aches from their muscles. There is a hole conveniently cut in the ice of the lake outside in which the brave may take a plunge and – more regularly used – a wood fire on which to toast sausages.

Food in Finland is substantial rather than delicate. Reindeer steaks, salmon, special cheeses and snowberries go down well with high proof Finnish Vodka.

Saunas are a part of everyday life in Finland. Every good hotel and block of apartments has one and the Finns seem quite surprised that anyone should be reluctant to take off all their clothes. In the advice given to competitors in the 50-mile Finlandia race, there is the suggestion not to spend too long in the sauna afterwards. With 9,000 competitors, say the organizers, all wanting the same refreshment, it could get pretty crowded!

A serious training center, where the Finnish racers go to get fit, is at Vuokatti, between the Arctic Circle and Helsinki. Set in deep forest, it has some quite difficult tracks which wind up and down a fairly steep hill crowned with a beacon. Happily for those just learning, there are easy trails, too, cut through the tall birches and across a small lake. Another ski center in central Finland is Viitasaari, where the Hotel Ruuponsaari offers swimming for adults and children, saunas, tennis and special child-minding and entertainment.

Each small settlement in Finland offers ski and boot hire. As this equipment is not expensive however, it is really better for visitors to bring their own, as the choice may well be limited. Note that Finns prefer to use wax on their skis rather than fur strips or fish scales. This makes the skis run better and, as the temperature in Finland is fairly constant, there are not the problems of constantly changing wax according to the warmer or colder conditions which occur in more southerly countries.

Finnish is quite different from the other Scandinavian languages. It is from the same root as Hungarian and is thought to be remotely linked to the Indo-European family of languages. Practically every Finn speaks Swedish as well as his own language and most speak English.

FACTS

Location
Helsinki, the capital of Finland, lies on the same altitude as the northern tip of Labrador, the Shetland Isles and Leningrad. The far North of Lapland is 720 miles from the capital, on a level with the North of Alaska.

Ski areas
The whole country is a ski area during the long winter. A large number of those which have been developed cluster round the Arctic Circle, apart from Helsinki itself. One of the most varied programs is at Kilpisjärvi in the far North West. The skiing is principally cross-country.

Accommodation
Hotels and hostels.

Activities
The ever-present sauna, maybe followed by a plunge into the water below the ice.

WORLD-WIDE SKIING

Australia

map
page 120

Australians are inveterate skiers. They find their way into ski resorts all over the world, picking up jobs on the piste patrol, as lift operators or disco organizers. So it is not surprising that even if their country does not offer the greatest natural resources in the powder and sunshine stakes, where there are mountains there is plenty of fun-loving skiing. The Snowy Mountains curl across the South East corner of the continent bringing ski fields within driving distance from Sydney, Melbourne and Canberra. The weather can be uncertain and July is the best month but often the season goes on from June to October.

Most of the ski areas started off with rope tows put up by groups of friends who formed themselves into clubs, built huts and gradually developed resorts. Now there are about a dozen areas with villages, chair lifts, pomas and a busy, if sometimes precarious winter season.

The South-Eastern resorts are divided between Victoria and New South Wales and development is at a critical stage just now. A recent Ski Industry of Victoria working party encouraged development in Victoria's four main residential resorts of Mount Buller, Mount Baw Baw, Falls Creek and Mount Hotham. Further development in New South Wales, on the contrary has been held back by the long awaited Kosciusko National Park Draft plan, and conservationists are hoping to prevent any building in its area. The slopes are crowded and hour-long lines cut down skiing time.

All the same, Thredbo, centrally situated between Melbourne and Sydney – just over 500 miles from either of them – is probably the busiest and best-developed area of Australia. There is a good village with chair lifts rising up a big bowl to around 6,500 ft. The skiing is very varied. Beginners have sheltered runs down Merritts Spur, and there is a long run down for intermediates here which leads to Creek. When there is powder about, it settles round Antons Peak. From the top of the new triple chair, Crackenback Falls is challenging, though better grooming has made it less lethal than it used to be. On the slopes, money has been spent on amenities. Eagles Nest restaurant provides fast food and, as they do in the Rockies, hosts and hostesses show skiers how to get the best from the slopes.

Perisher does not have such a big area as Thredbo but its snow tends to be more reliable and of better quality, and it is a popular center: 150 instructors work there, at Australia's biggest ski school. The runs are short but offer plenty of variety from easy glades through the gum trees to short sharp mogul slopes. One area around the Valley Inn Hotel is fairly easy; the other on Mount Perisher has Olympic and Eyre lifts for the more exprt. Like Thredbo, the rough edges are being smoothed, slopes are being groomed and money is being put into the new Perisher Centre to improve facilities for skiers. Close to Perisher is Smiggin Holes, another small ski area.

Victoria bustles with an atmosphere of exciting growth. Mount Stirling, near Mount Buller, and another completely new area in the State are marked out for development as major resorts of international standard.

Mount Buller is less than three hours drive from Melbourne and has a lively village set round Bourke Street, which is a useful nursery area. A big new car park and two triple chair lifts are helping to cope with the crowds which come up at weekends. A new small area on Little Buller Spur also helps to spread the load and lengthen the intermediate runs. The area is still growing. Those who can stay through the week, enjoy quiet slopes and lively evening entertainment for there are plenty of restaurants and discos.

Mount Hotham features a new triple chair lift and a poma at the top for beginners – they can come back down by chair. Intermediate slopes and sheltered skiing among the gum trees is being expanded and the real estate business is booming with apartments for sale and rental; eight new club lodges have been built. Mount Hotham's capacity will shortly be doubled to 7,000 beds. It is 367 miles from Melbourne;

Location	**Ski areas**	**Accommodation**
The Snowy Mountain range which crosses New South Wales and Victoria.	Considerable development at Mount Buller, Mount Baw Baw, Falls Creek and Mount Hotham. Other resorts by Mount Kosciusko (7,316 ft), Thredbo (up to 6,500 ft), Perisher and Smiggin Hole. The season is June to October.	Generally, a good range of apartments and club lodges.

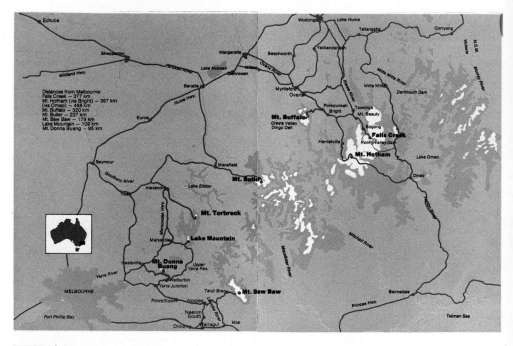

Distances from Melbourne:
Falls Creek — 377 km
Mt. Hotham (via Bright) — 367 km
(via Omeo) — 488 km
Mt. Buffalo — 320 km
Mt. Buller — 237 km
Mt. Baw Baw — 179 km
Lake Mountain — 109 km
Mt. Donna Buang — 95 km

AUSTRALIA

Sydney skiers fly to Albury and pick up the coach service which runs from there.

The Snowy Mountains are made of very old rock and age has worn them into gently rounded shapes unlike the jagged peaks of the Rockies or Alps. The wind whistles across them – Perisher can earn its name – but the gum trees spread their umbrella shapes across the slopes to give shelter. It is a country where energy, toughness and young enthusiasm are needed – and that just about sums up the Australian character.

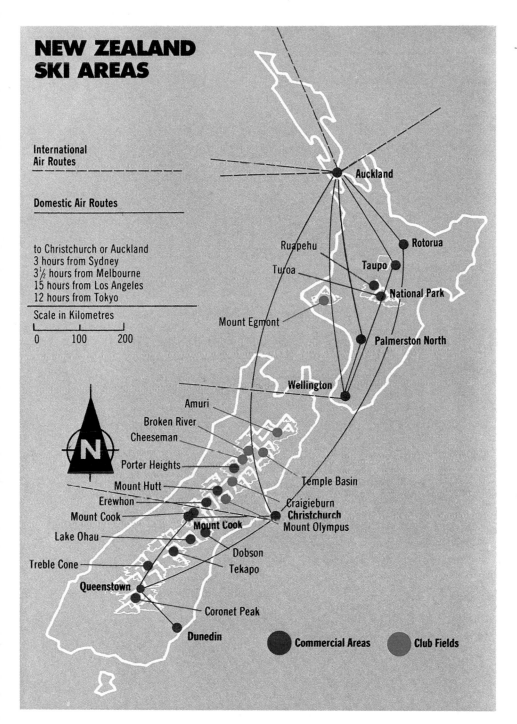

NEW ZEALAND SKI AREAS

International Air Routes

Domestic Air Routes

to Christchurch or Auckland
3 hours from Sydney
3½ hours from Melbourne
15 hours from Los Angeles
12 hours from Tokyo

Scale in Kilometres
0   100   200

Auckland

Ruapehu
Turoa
Rotorua
Taupo
National Park

Mount Egmont

Palmerston North

Wellington

Amuri
Broken River
Cheeseman
Porter Heights
Mount Hutt
Erewhon
Mount Cook
Lake Ohau
Treble Cone
Queenstown

Temple Basin
Craigieburn
Christchurch
Mount Olympus

Mount Cook

Dobson
Tekapo

Coronet Peak

Dunedin

Commercial Areas   Club Fields

WORLD-WIDE SKIING

New Zealand

maps
*pages 121,
124*

New Zealand's pioneering days are over so far as the snow is concerned. Skiing was first organized by groups of friends who formed a club, then struggled up tracks to the mountain slopes, built their own club huts and brought up temporary rope tows. Club fields still exist and skiers can still backpack into remote areas, find a hut and cook for themselves. There are also at least a dozen commercially developed resorts provided with chair lifts, day lodges, snow grooming machines and ski schools.

The building of villages on the slopes has been discouraged, so that visitors usually stay some way from the skiing, driving up precipitous roads to reach the snow. Big car parks greet them on the brink of the slopes and then there is often a hike on foot up to the first lift.

The mountain area is vast. The alps of North Island and South Island are greater in extent than those of central Eurode. There are no trees on the ski slopes but they are far from featureless, for the volcanic ring which circles the Pacific passes right through North Island and gives a unique character to the landscape. Some cones slowly spew great glaciers; in other places hot springs gush from underground. After a hard day on the slopes a dip in a thermal pool relaxes the tensions of stiff muscles.

North Island – about the same distance from the South Pole as Nevada or Greece from the North Pole – rises in the center to New Zealand's highest mountain, Mount Ruapehu. Turoa, one of New Zealand's latest developments, lies on its south-western slopes. The chair lifts and tows reach the highest point of the country at over 7,600 ft. As well as a good 2½-mile run and several pistes, there is a nursery area which machines keep well groomed. Three cafés show that there is plenty of custom on the slopes. The developers have come up with a novel solution to the accommodation problem. Ohakune, the nearest town, is ten miles from the slopes, but it has a caravan center for 100 4-berth caravans for weekenders.

The Whakapapa resort is also on Mount Ruapehu. Skiers stay at

FACTS

Location
Mount Ruapehu.

Resorts
Turoa (7,600 ft) and Whakapapa. The season is from late June to early October.

Accommodation
It is common to drive out of the large towns and ski for the day, so the full range of hotels in Auckland and Wellington is available. Turoa is served specifically by caravans.

SOUTH ISLAND

Resorts
Coronet Peak (up to 5,200 ft), close by Queenstown. Mount Hutt, served by the ski village of Methven, close by Christchurch. And the resort of Tekapo. The season is from June to late November.

Activities
Heliskiing on the Tasman Glacier.

Chateau-in-the-Sky, a big lodge only five miles from the slopes, and buses take them to and fro. As Whakapapa is right between Auckland and Wellington, it has the benefits and problems of being New Zealand's busiest resort. There is money to provide facilities but lines tend to build up at times. There is a vertical drop of 3,000 ft over three miles of slopes but the season is short, lasting from late June until early October.

On South Island, nearer the Pole, the snow lasts from June to November or even early December and there are three main resorts, each with its own atmosphere and clientele.

Mogul addicts enjoy the short steep slopes of Coronet Peak where two well separated chair lifts rise to above 5,200 ft. For those who need instruction on gentler slopes there is a separate nursery area. Classes, both for beginners and better skiers, are kept small and there is video for those who want to see themselves in action on the slopes. International racers come here for slaloms and giant slaloms each May, when the European and American circuits are closed.

After a day on the slopes at South Island's Coronet Peak, skiers return to Queenstown ten miles off, to dance and dine in the nearest thing to the atmosphere of après-ski in New Zealand. There are several top class hotels and a variety of good restaurants.

International races are also held at Mount Hutt and here there is room for downhill courses. The season, usually the longest in the Southern Alps, lasts from May to December. From Christchurch, skiers drive 65 miles across the beautiful Canterbury Plains, or there are chalets and hotels in the small village of Methven at the bottom of the mountain. Local radio gives daily snow reports and the area is lucky in being sheltered from the northern warmth and rain which sometimes bring mist and damp to North Island. Mount Hutt rises in a big open bowl from the day lodge with double T-bars, rope tows and pomas.

There is a small but well equipped area at Tekapo. The village is a summer township 20 miles from the slopes and skiers travel by coach or ski plane. The plane has the advantage of landing skiers high above the main area, so they start with a breathtaking descent to the lifts.

One of the most exciting experiences is the regular ski-plane and helicopter service to the Tasman Glacier. The helicopters take off eight miles from Mount Cook, landing their passengers high on the glacier to find steep powder bowls and the long gentle tour down the icy snout. There is no ski school: the authorities say that if a skier needs lessons he has no business to be there. It is an expert's area. Groups are kept small and well guided.

The great mountain ranges of the southern alps are well on their way to becoming a winter sports center for the sports-keen Australians and New Zealanders. The snow and enthusiasm have always been there, now the lifts, schools, hire shops and restaurants are opening up. The problems of accommodation and transport arise out of respect for great wilderness areas and they are overcome by the friendly goodwill of the people who still have a club rather than a commercial approach to their precious snow fields.

following page Turoa, Mount Hutt, maps ▶

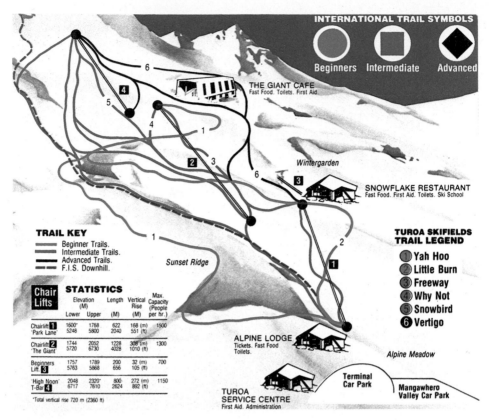

INTERNATIONAL TRAIL SYMBOLS

Beginners | Intermediate | Advanced

THE GIANT CAFE
Fast Food. Toilets. First Aid.

Wintergarden

SNOWFLAKE RESTAURANT
Fast Food. First Aid. Toilets. Ski School

TRAIL KEY
Beginner Trails.
Intermediate Trails.
Advanced Trails.
F.I.S. Downhill.

Sunset Ridge

TUROA SKIFIELDS TRAIL LEGEND
1 Yah Hoo
2 Little Burn
3 Freeway
4 Why Not
5 Snowbird
6 Vertigo

Chair Lifts — STATISTICS

Chair Lifts	Elevation (M) Lower	Elevation (M) Upper	Length (M)	Vertical Rise (M)	Max. Capacity (People per hr.)
Chairlift 1 'Park Lane'	1600* 5248	1768 5800	622 2040	168 (m) 551 (ft)	1500
Chairlift 2 'The Giant'	1744 5720	2052 6730	1228 4028	308 (m) 1010 (ft)	1300
Beginners Lift 3	1757 5763	1789 5868	200 656	32 (m) 105 (ft)	700
'High Noon' T-Bar 4	2048 6717	2320* 7610	800 2624	272 (m) 892 (ft)	1150

*Total vertical rise 720 m (2360 ft)

ALPINE LODGE
Tickets. Fast Food. Toilets.

Alpine Meadow

TUROA SERVICE CENTRE
First Aid. Administration

Terminal Car Park

Mangawhero Valley Car Park

TUROA ▲

1 Two parallel Lower Doppelmayr T-Bar Lifts.
2 Two parallel Upper Doppelmayr T-Bar Lifts.
3 Planned treble Chairlift.
4 Huber Chalet site.
5 South Peak of Mount Hutt 2075 metres (6810 feet) above sea level.
6 Two fixed grid learners lifts.
7 Public Day Lodge, ski hire shop, cafeteria.
8 Toilets.
9 Car Park.
10 Doppelmayr Platter lift for advanced beginners.
11 Doppelmayr Platter lift for intermediate skiers.
12 Ski School office.

SKI TRAILS
◆ Advanced. Most difficult.
■ Intermediate. More difficult.
○ Learners. Easiest.

MOUNT HUTT ▲

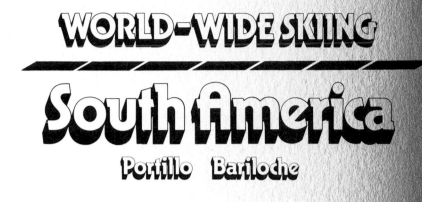

South America
Portillo Bariloche

The great backbone of the Andes stretches down the West side of South America, concealing hundreds of potential ski resorts in its unexplored ranges. More than a dozen have been built, of which two, Portillo in Chile and Bariloche in Argentina are the best known. Both are on the southern hemisphere circuit for international racers. Portillo hosted a world championship as long ago as 1966 and the International Ski Federation held a congress at Bariloche in 1977.

The main problem in South America is the difficulty of communications. Argentina is a vast country, stretching from subtropical rain forests in the North down to the frozen wastes of the Antarctic. Although the distances across are considerably shorter than those from North to South, Buenos Aires is nearly 30 hours by bus or rail from Bariloche. A third of Argentina's population lives in the capital city and those who want to ski usually have to fly there. Bariloche is untouched by the political problems which have dogged Argentina for decades. The only danger at night is the possibility of falling into potholes caused by the continual roadworks.

Bariloche is undergoing transformation, and several thousand beds are being added to the little town. It is already a surprising mixture of European and American. Much of the population originally came from Austria and Germany, so many of the hotels have Alpine names and character. Yet the council chamber and wooden houses which cluster along the shores of the great lake Narwal Huapi, have an Indian character and are unlike anything one would find in the Alps.

The lake is spectacular, especially when great banks of cloud roll over the surrounding hills. Excursions can be made by steamer to islands where little deer, wild boar and other game run freely. Behind Bariloche, in the foothills of the Andes, there are *estancias* where cattle and sheep graze on the thin grass in the summer, and condors wheel overhead.

The slopes of the Cerro Cathedral mountain are a 12-mile bus ride away. There are cablecars going up to 6,500 ft and chair lifts and tows making up a good network. A three-mile-long run from the top starts on steep open slopes, ending where bushes dot the lower slopes. There are nursery areas both at the bottom of the lifts and half-way up. The summit of Cerro Cathedral is over 11,000 ft, so there is plenty of room for development and wonderful untouched slopes all around.

Portillo, in Chile, is better placed than Bariloche, as it lies only 80 miles from Santiago but there, too, communications can break down when snow falls so heavily that it blocks all traffic. The resort lies high, at 9,300 ft and set in the bottom of a great open bowl is the Gran Hotel Portillo. Mountains rise all round, reaching to the high point in the southern hemisphere, Mount Aconcagua, at 22,834 ft.

The season lasts from May to the end of October and many of the racing teams from the North come to Portillo to train, even if not to race during these months. The Roca Jack is definitely for experts only but there are easier slopes too, and a good ski school.

Further development of the Andes for tourists will, one day, open up a superb area for skiers.

FACTS

Location
The Andes range.

PORTILLO, CHILE
Resort at 9,300 ft, surrounded by ski areas up to Mount Aconcagua at 22,834 ft. The season is from May to late October.

BARILOCHE, ARGENTINA
There is a resort area around Cerro Cathedral, with ski areas from 6,500 ft up to 11,000 ft. Plentiful accommodation.

WHAT KIND OF SKIING

Beginners

Watch a World Cup downhill on television and it seems so very easy to sweep down the smooth slopes, edging swiftly sideways round the corners, tucking down the straights and descending a whole mountainside while hundredths of seconds flicker away.

Watch a beginner losing balance on a gentle slope, struggling with long planks which seem determined to go their separate ways and the conclusion is obvious. Skiing is not so easy. It must be learnt.

Fortunately even the learning is fun right from the outset. For one thing it is not a solitary business. Skiing is taught in classes and while learning the skier also gets to know a whole group of new people. Sharing the problems of staying upright and getting up again after the twentieth fall, or facing together the first ski tow or a particularly steep slope, can bring a ski class together in the same spirit as a boat crew during a gale at sea.

Then the ski instructors — handsome, tanned and incredibly agile on their skis — remind their pupils that skis really can be mastered and the occasional schnapps on the mountain and a badge at a ski school evening at the end of the week give extra encouragement.

Since the turn of the century there have been ski schools. In the early nineteen hundreds, Mathias Zdarsky ran one at Lilienfeld in Austria where he taught how to control speed and direction with the use of a single, diskless pole. Hannes Schneider took over the Arlberg School at St Anton in 1922 and built it into the greatest in the world.

Arlberg instructors went to America in the forties and fifties and started schools in the many resorts which were developing at that time. They naturally took with them the Austrian technique. Back in Europe, however, each country was developing its national ski school and each had its own method. The result was that bewildered recreational skiers would learn one method in one country and then spend half the next holiday unlearning it. Counter rotation, christiania legere, the jargon multiplied without helping the skier on his way down the mountain safely and swiftly.

Then Interski started, a biennial meeting of ski instructors from every country at which methods were discussed and demonstrated. Gradually the teaching methods were co-ordinated and a more natural system evolved.

Then, simultaneously in America and France, two men invented a way of teaching beginners on very short skis. Lessons begin on skis three feet long; after a couple of days the student graduates to four-and-a-half feet and so on up to regular length. Clif Taylor in Colorado called this the graduated length method (GLM) and Robert Blanc in Les Arcs called it *ski evolutif*. No longer was it necessary for skiers to learn the snow plough turn of the Arlberg method. They could keep their feet together and skis parallel, making skiing less tiring and more elegant.

Long skis were still needed by good skiers wanting to go fast, for the length gives directional stability for straight skiing. But gradually improvements in ski manufacture and especially the development of various polyurethane mixes in the construction of skis gave short ones the same stability as the old long ones. Most skis are now made of layers sandwiched together and the twisting and vibration can be controlled.

Short skis can be turned more easily among moguls or heavy, cut-up snow. On them a beginner can set off confidently down a gentle slope after a few minutes practice. A day or two later, the beginner is progressing to ski lifts and easy runs. Often the climax to two weeks of ski school is a ride to a nearby mountain to come down a whole mountain side – though this may take an afternoon rather than a World Cup winning two minutes.

It is always possible to learn more about skiing. After mastering the easy slopes there are steeper or more uneven ones to tackle. Swinging parallel down a smooth piste is only a stage less breathtaking than mastering a stretch of moguls. Best of all is untracked snow. The deep powder that comes so regularly to the Rockies adds a sense of exhilaration as it spurts up under the skis. But skiing powder needs special technique.

Snow conditions are not always perfect and great skill and experience go into finding the best way down the mountain. Breakable crust, built up by sun and frost alternating, must be mastered or avoided. So must ice. Only by touring often with a guide will a skier learn how to avoid the dangers of crevasses and avalanche slopes and how to find the best powder or spring snow.

Racing is a technique of its own and needs to be learned early. By the time they reach ten-years-old, racers-to-be are spending all their vacations on the snow, learning the intricacies of slalom, downhill or giant slalom and building the right muscles with fitness training. Ex-racers find a further challenge in free style. The complicated leaps, twists and somersaults off vertiginous jumps are practised into water which is specially aerated to make awkward landings as soft as possible. Then, like a butterfly shedding its chrysalis, the free styler changes wetsuit for brightly colored skisuit and graduates to the snow.

Even the instructors are always learning. The Swiss ski school runs a course for its instructors each December. It takes place in a big resort such as Crans-Montana, Davos or Grindelwald. Skiers are needed as guinea pigs to be taught, so they are given special rates for accommodation and instruction. This is the way to prepare for the season. All the previous year's mistakes can be corrected and by the time the course is over every muscle is in trim for the coming season.

Many of the high resorts where snow is sure to come in November open with pre season courses at reduced rates to persuade skiers to fill the slopes and the beds at what would otherwise be a very empty time. Skiers who cannot get to the mountains at these times will find the same sort of courses, in a more limited way, going on at artificial ski slopes at home.

Looking back at one's first days on skis it is easy to forget that it was possible to enjoy trying to remember to shift weight, plant poles, bend knees. But right from the start the friendly rivalry of the classes and the occasional achievement of a perfect turn make it all worthwhile. Whether it is tackling the first straight *schuss* down a gentle slope or searching for perfect snow away in the wilderness, learning brings one satisfaction after another.

WHAT KIND OF SKIING

Heliskiing in Canada

For over a century those who wanted to enjoy
skiing down mountain slopes had to climb them first. Admittedly, there
were a few mountain railways in Switzerland which were conveniently
sited so that skiers could use them to reach higher slopes and then
ski down. The building of lifts purely for the convenience of skiers
began slowly, and seeing cablecars, chairs and tows surround every
resort, nowadays it is difficult to believe how recently a brief schuss
had to be preceded by hours of humping skis uphill.

But progress being what it is, there is a growing breed of skier who
today demands to travel far and fast down the slopes and the remoter
mountains without waiting in lines for slow lifts. For him or her
helicopters and light planes are the answer. They can whisk skiers up
from valley to mountain top in a matter of minutes, leave them to ski
down thousands of feet of untracked snow, then pick them up again as
they reach the bottom and fly them to another range of fresh snow.

In many areas of the world it is possible, even though expensive, to
hire a helicopter for a small group of people. In France helicopters are
banned except for emergency use but many resorts in other Alpine
countries provide them on a regular basis. More remote areas of the
world, such as the Tasman glacier in the southern hemisphere and
Alaska in the north, have mountain guides and helicopters ready to
explore huge regions which may never be developed into ski resorts.
The most famous of all areas – one which has become synonymous with
heliskiing – is in the Rocky Mountains of British Columbia, Canada,
especially the Cariboos, Bugaboos and Monashees.

The scheme was started by Hans Gmoser who founded Canadian
Mountain Holidays in 1965. He invited eighteen guests to try heliskiing
in the Cariboo mountains. At the time his staff consisted of one pilot,
one cook and one guide. Now 3,500 skiers a year pour into several
areas; large Bell helicopters spend each day ferrying groups up the
mountains; lodges have been built high on the slopes and there is

constant radio communication among aircraft and bases from Panorama in the South to Valemount more than 250 miles North in British Columbia. Every year the areas are extended and expert skiers from all over the world fly in to achieve what to them is a supreme form of skiing.

The mountain ranges are so vast that there is room for everyone without overlapping. In the Cariboos alone there are twelve distinct skiing areas ranging from wide open gentle glacier runs to steep demanding tree glades. After Hans Gmoser have come other operators, such as Mike Wiegele, who helicopters his guests into the Cariboos and Monashees from Blue River. Mountain Canada offers day trips in the Purcell and Selkirk ranges.

One of the benefits of South-Western Canada is its usually stable weather, though heliski organizers guarantee nothing. They go out of their way to explain that conditions can be 'the worst imaginable'. After all, snow must fall as the basis of the whole operation but skiers are unlucky if more than a day or two in a week are spoilt by bad conditions.

With a helicopter as uphill transport, a skier can easily achieve 60,000 ft of vertical drop in a day but the physical demands are enormous. It is essential to be a fit and competent skier. Exercises are sternly recommended for those whose lives generally keep them behind office desks with breaks only for business lunches. Pre heliski courses are also suggested and it is not a bad idea to go to an area where days of strenuous non-stop skiing can be alternated with easier days using the lifts.

Banff Ski Club, in Canada, organize trial weeks and at the new resort of Panorama near the Purcell range all the facilities of a normal village are being built. There are lifts, bars, restaurants, a discotheque and a ski shop with condominiums set round a 'village' square, though heliskiing is the principal attraction. Another excellent warm-up is a week further South in the Wasatch mountains of Utah, to get used to skiing in deep powder, to get fit and, as many skiers come from across the world, to get over jetlag.

Heliski organizers put extreme emphasis on safety. Each group has a qualified guide who is an expert in mountain rescue and medical aid. He must also know the mountains and be a strong, competent skier. He carries any equipment which may be necessary if a helicopter is prevented by bad weather from rescuing a group which has encountered trouble. Everyone in the group carries an avalanche rescue transceiver strapped to them and before setting out on their first flight they learn how to use them to find buried skiers. The guides take regular refresher courses in hazard evaluation and stabilization, weather observation and snowcraft. Like the people they lead, they come from all over the world; tough young men born in the mountains of Switzerland, Austria, France, and Italy as well as South and North America, Australia and New Zealand.

In some areas the skiers stay in small Canadian towns or at motels conveniently sited along the highways, by railways or near airports but the best mountain lodges are up on the slopes and can be reached only by helicopter.

They are, however, built with every comfort, including whirlpools and saunas, massage and – always a feature of heliski tours – delicious and plentiful food. Most have shops to sell the essentials their clients may not bring: short, soft skis, ski poles with safety straps which break apart, and overalls, goggles and gaiters all built to keep out the penetrating powder which is so fine that it sifts into ordinary clothing.

The prices of heliskiing vacations are high, even if they do not include a transatlantic or Pacific flight. They must include the costs of helicopters, fuel, pilots, guides and mountain lodges. But if the charges are calculated in the cost per foot of downhill skiing then they become very low indeed.

The morning routine starts at daybreak; breakfast is hearty, then comes the strict discipline of the helicopter. The pilots have to be as skilled as the guides for it is upon them that many lives depend and they have the same authority as a captain at sea. Skiers learn the drill of approaching from the front of the helicopter, going aboard by numbers and clipping themselves in. The machine whirs into action, lofts and wheels around with the ground first dropping away, then slipping along quickly underneath. At the chosen slope the machine comes down for the first drop of the day and, without delay, the skiers jump out with their skis and crouch down. The helicopter revs up to ascend, spurting snow over the huddled figures. As it disappears to pick up the next group, the skiers clip into their bindings and set off.

Across the wide slopes they space out, making long curling ribbons across vast tracts of mountain, gasping as the light snow ripples up over knees, waist and shoulders, until they all but disappear in it. The powder sifts into open mouths and flickers across goggles and there is no sensation left but of going down, down, down.

Hundreds of feet further on they reach the tree line and come closer together as they plunge through the pines, twisting and turning. They reach the bottom with muscles aching, lungs panting, blood tingling. Within minutes the helicopter appears overhead, hovers a moment, sends up the now familiar stinging cloud of snow and drops softly to pick them up.

If it is fine at the end of the morning, lunch is brought out and eaten in a sunny, sheltered spot. If it is snowing, everyone comes back to the lodge or hotel for lunch and goes out again to be dropped just above the trees where it is easier to see.

In a week a strong skier can achieve 200,000 vertical feet of downhill skiing. If even more excitement is demanded, then there are ridges to turn across, rock drop-offs, steep chutes and great natural bumps to jump off. This is the ultimate in skiing for the fit, the dedicated and the brave.

UNITED STATES OF AMERICA

New York North of
_____

Utah
_____

Lake Tahoe
_____

Alaska
_____

Colorado

UNITED STATES OF AMERICA

North of New York

Wherever there are mountains close to cities and the weather temperature drops in winter, people are ready to spend money and energy turning slopes into ski runs, even though nature may not be so helpful as she is in the great ski areas. The sun may shine more brilliantly in New Mexico; the panorama of peaks may be more awe-inspiring from Crans Montana but for someone living in Manhattan, it is easier to spend a weekend in Hunter Mountain.

Until recently one huge question mark lay over every season and held back development. Skiers can ski without the sun; downhill addicts can make do with crosscountry trails if the terrain is flat, but one commodity cannot be dispensed with – snow. Fortunately man's ingenuity has even managed to overcome nature's occasional failure to supply the white crystals. Snow guns can be relied upon to coat the trails back down to the village. Great heaps can be built up on cold nights to spread over bare patches when necessary. The stuff they produce is more than just acceptable as a substitute. Even the top ski racers of the world were complimentary about the courses manufactured on Whiteface Mountain for the 1980 Olympics. Hunter Mountain, only 100 miles from New York City, can cover the whole of its skiable acreage with manmade snow.

Even with the certainty of snow, few people fly in from far away to take a long holiday in the Eastern mountains. Just as in Scotland and Australia, skiers there often have to put up with icy slopes and wet winds. True, there are days when clear blue skies following a snowfall bring the most pampered skier out on the slopes but Easterners are generally known to be tough. They do not complain about the need for all-weather clothing. Some of them buy second homes in established resorts but most of the traffic comes at weekends.

There are three kinds of Eastern skiers: those who go out for the day or weekend to the many small resorts (New York State alone has over 80); those who have convenient second homes in pretty New England villages; and those who take their exercise wandering crosscountry through the wilderness.

On winter weekends when the forecast is good, hundreds of city dwellers crowd the highways leading to the hills. As well as Hunter Mountain, Catamount is only two hours drive from New York City. There's a 1,000 ft vertical drop there and at night the lights are lit so that skiing can go on after sunset. For resorts further away, the trick is to fly to a regional airport and pick up a skierized car equipped with snow tires, ski rack and extra antifreeze to cover the last few miles. Gore Mountain is a good example just 33 miles from Glen Falls airport. Green Peak is serviced by Syracuse airport. With so many spots to choose from, new territory can be explored each weekend. During the week the slopes are quieter, lines disappear and prices drop sharply.

Another type of resort are those where families settle into condominiums during weeks of school vacations. By far the most famous is Lake Placid, which hosted the Winter Olympics in 1932 and 1980. In 1932 the Winter Games consisted only of Nordic ski events and skating. By 1980 Whiteface Mountain was able to provide steep slaloms and a superb downhill course down 3,216 vertical ft. Six chair lifts and tows cover the 28 trails and, thanks to the Olympics, there are three lodges on the mountainside.

The town itself is 12 miles from Whiteface and its pretty painted wood houses are charmingly set round the lake where snow mobiles take visitors on joyrides. Should the weather close in on Whiteface, the facilities provided for other Olympic sports can be thrilling. Even to climb up the great 233 ft and 295 ft jumping hills and peep down the sheer icy chutes which lead to thin air would be thrill enough for most people. The bobrun is also there to be tested – with a professional driver and brakeman to stop nasty spills. Passengers hurtle down the walls, hanging upside down as centrifugal force presses the bobsleighs up against the great curves. The great ice arena echoes to the memory of Britain's Robin Cousins, Russia's pair skaters Irina Rodnina and Alexander Zaitsev and the triumphant United States ice hockey team.

The Olympic crosscountry trails start at Mount van Hoevenburg, on the outskirts of Lake Placid. The trails were cut to test the experts but there is plenty of scope for punters too.

Many well equipped and comfortable resorts have grown up in New England. The pretty town of Stowe in Vermont, with its clapboard houses, redwood barns and white steeples, is one such center. There is challenging skiing on nearby Mount Mansfield, easier trails on Spruce peak, and beginners learn on the Toll House slopes. The newer and elegant Sugarbush is also in Vermont, and much used by city businessmen, who take comfortable condominiums. Well-groomed trails flatter their skiing and there are more than 20 excellent restaurants, as well as jacuzzis, indoor tennis, heated pools and saunas for the time spent off the slopes. In New Hampshire, Waterville Valley is a good example of a quiet and friendly area set among birch and larch with a fairly easy ski area on Mount Tecumseh.

Right across the range of high rolling hills that stretch between New York City and the Canadian frontier there are, in spite of the density of population, great wilderness areas. Many are protected, like the Green Mountain Forest, and the Adirondack and Catskill parks. But even in the areas where skilift pylons and piste beating machines are anathema,

FACTS

Weekend ski areas
Hunter Mountains, two hours drive from New York City. Catamount, also two hours drive away. Gore Mountains, 33 miles from Glen Falls airport. There are over 80 small resorts in New York State, often hardly used during the week.

Vacation resorts
Lake Placid, serving Whiteface Mountain and Mount van Hoevenburg. Stowe and Sugarbush in Vermont.

Crosscountry
The wilderness areas towards the Canadian frontier contain tough crosscountry skiing and lodges or hotels for overnighting. The areas include Green Mountain Forest, and the Adirondack and Catskill Parks.

there are trails once used by garnet miners, Indians and trappers. Along these hikers and backpackers now pick their ways in summer and crosscountry skiers move swiftly through in winter.

Lodges vary from well-equipped hotels to simple farmhouses, where backpackers stretch out their sleeping bags in attics and hang all they can carry on a hook overnight. The trails are well marked. Some prefer to base themselves on a single lodge while others travel from one to another. Guides are always available and often talks by naturalists and ski experts help to pass the evenings by open fires. Rip van Winkle may have slept away the decades in the Catskills but today's skiers go there to keep fit and young. Compasses and maps are more useful than cassette players along the trails and insulation and heat retention govern the choice of clothes rather than the latest dictates of the fashion weeklies.

There is as much variety in New England's ski areas as there is in the people who work in its big cities. Those who want to be carried up the slopes in comfortable gondolas and try carving their turns down well-groomed trails can do so. Those who prefer to wander along trails frequented by small woodland animals, carrying with them all they need to survive, are just as happy. There was a time when facilities were sparse because they were used only when the snow came. Now that man can insure a season of several months it is worth erecting skilifts, opening restaurants, building condominiums to satisfy the urge to ski.

UNITED STATES OF AMERICA

Utah

Park City   Deer Valley
Snow Bird   Alta

maps
pages 137,
140, 141

left
**Snowpacking
crews and
machinery
keep the
slopes in top
condition in
Snowbird**

In the 1860's it was mining that brought prosperity to the area around Salt Lake City and still the atmosphere of the old mines lingers in names like Claimjumper and Prospector for trails, Cold Miners Daughter and Iron Blosam for lodges. Stark outlines of derelict workings remain within sight of busy mountain restaurants.

DEER VALLEY SKI FACTS
New resort will boast 20 lifts serving
more than 80 runs for all grades –

By the end of the century, the minerals were no longer worth working and now it is snow, with the tourists it attracts, which have revitalized the old villages.

Alta, perhaps the most famous of the resorts, enjoys an average 500 inches of snow a year of a special quality. It comes in great storms which sweep across the Nevada desert bringing crystals which are very dry and fluffy. As the skier plunges down the steep mountainside the light powder ripples up. 'Keep your mouth shut' is a common warning, for a deep breath can take the powder straight into the lungs. The deep light layer forms the most exhilarating of all surfaces in which to ski and nature renews it every few days through a season that lasts from mid November to early May. There are twelve ski areas within 55 miles of Salt Lake City and all of them benefit to some extent from this particularly good snow.

Park City is the resort which probably suits beginners and intermediates best. Its gondola lift is the longest in the West. The cabins, which hold four people, rise 2,400 ft from the resort at 6,900 ft. To supplement them there are nine double and two triple chair lifts. The trails are beaten up to 10,000 ft and in the Scott and Jupiter bowls near the top lies the famous light powder. Down the sides of the bowls are short steep trails for expert skiers. There is even one area, the Hoist, kept for those who use skis of 190 cm (over 5 ft) or longer, so that the moguls stay big and round rather than cut up by intermediate skiers' short skis. Beginners learn by the graduated length method and have a well segregated nursery area round First Time and Three Kings lifts. Intermediates have plenty of broad, well-groomed trails about three-and-a-half miles long. Those who never tire use one long trail, Payday, which is lit every night of the week until 10 pm.

Although Main Street, the resort and the lodges are scattered, there is a free bus service which runs regularly during the day and evening to link them.

The atmosphere of the silver mines (it is still possible to visit a working mine at Park City) colors the night life. The Main Street of the old village lies just two miles from the foot of the gondola and the restaurants and bars which line it are reminiscent of life a hundred years ago. Bluegrass music pours out through the saloon doors and there is always the feeling that the ghosts of silver miners are not far away.

The restaurants – and there are over forty of them – serve every kind of food from Mexican and Japanese to Italian and Irish. Potato John's, as well as providing food, will video a group's progress on the slopes during the day, play it back in the evening, and sell the tape if the group is proud enough of its performances to want to buy.

In Park City, as in all the resorts and towns of the Mormon State, drink is subject to special laws but that does not mean the town is dry. Bottles (discreetly hidden in brown bags) can be bought at State Liquor Stores and taken into restaurants. Some beer and wine can usually be bought with meals and many bars operate a membership system. This means that once a $5 fee has been paid members can buy liquor.

Just a few miles from Park City a new area, Deer Valley is being opened up and one day the two will join through lifts and trails. Typical

FACTS

Location
The old mining regions encircling Salt Lake City. There are 12 ski areas within 55 miles of the town, all well served by lifts.

Accommodation
Apart from accommodation in the resorts, it is easy to stay in Salt Lake City and drive out from there.

PARK CITY
Resort at 2,400 ft with trails beaten to 10,000 ft. Suitable for beginners and intermediates but with steep trails for experts. Loud and vigorous night life in the bars and restaurants of this old mining village.

FACTS

DEER VALLEY area

Two villages under development: Snow Park (7,200 ft) and Silver Lake (8,100 ft). Gentle trails and steep pitches, which lead to Bald Mountain (9,400 ft) and Bald Eagle (8,400 ft). Accommodation in condominiums and chalets.

SNOWBIRD

New resort built at 7,900 ft, rising to 11,000 ft. Tough skiing and untracked snow. Some night life in the bars of the lodges.

ALTA

Famous 1930s resort for all standards of skier but with particularly good steep runs. Limited accommodation in lodges and condominiums and quiet evenings.

of the very best ski resorts that are now being developed in the United States, Deer Valley is profiting from all the knowledge collected over the last half-century of ski resort construction. Two villages are being built, Snow Park at 7,200 ft and Silver Lake at 8,100 ft. Snow making on the lower slopes keeps them open right through the season.

Stein Eriksen, the Norwegian racer who won a gold medal for slalom in the 1952 Olympics and was Combined world champion in 1954, has laid out superb trails in Deer Valley through the aspen forests which reach to the top of Flagstaff, Bald and Bald Eagle Mountains. Steep pitches are linked with gentler ones; the trails are cut wide enough for intermediates to traverse across and islands of trees break up the motorway effect and conserve the snow.

The architecture is a mixture of modern, practical American with old-fashioned, practical European. Pitched roofs and deep eaves make sense when snow falls so deep. Two or three stories of woodcovered chalets fit more comfortably into a mountain landscape than tower blocks of concrete.

Development will be gradual over a twelve-year period, opening with the skiing on Bald Mountain and Bald Eagle Mountain, which reach up to 9,400 ft and 8,400 ft. The whole aim has been to provide a relaxed setting in which to spend a holiday. The village is an easy journey from a major airport. Familiar looking chalets nestle among the trees. Inside, the architecture, fittings and decoration have been designed to be easy on the eye and bones of a weary skier. The number of skiers allowed on the mountain will be restricted and the lifts are so sited that no lines will form. The North and North West orientation of the slopes will preserve the driest, lightest snow. Once a condominium or a vacation has been paid for, Deer Valley will provide a freedom from stress that will make it the envy of all skiers.

Snowbird, also only 45 minutes drive from Salt Lake City, lies in Little Cottonwood Canyon. It was built only ten years ago on an empty mountainside. Unique in the region, it has a tram which rises from 7,900 ft to 11,000 ft, holding 125 passengers. The skiing can be tough, as for instance on the Regulator Johnson trail which drops 1,100 ft over steep bump runs. Five double chair lifts link with the tram to serve 32 trails. Some lead through open bowls; others are cut through the great pines, which grow far enough apart to lure the powder hounds to slalom through them. The Wasatch Powderbird Guides lead those who love untracked snow on tours away from the prepared trails, sometimes using helicopters to open up new terrain.

Snowbird is a modern, efficiently run resort. Hosts and hostesses are prepared twice a day to take groups of newcomers on a tour of the slopes, and to help them make the most of the trails and lifts according to their ability. Lodges are clean and comfortable on the mountain and food is inexpensive and wholesome. The lift pass is half the cost of those for New England resorts. Processions and fun races are organized to entertain visitors and the children have their own easy Chickadee lift, complete with cartoon characters.

Night life is limited mainly to the bars in the lodges, of which the Eagles Nest in Cliff Lodge is the most comfortably equipped. There is one nightclub, The Tram Room, which operates either as a disco or

SNOWBIRD SKI FACTS
Mid-November to early May ski season, yearly average 450 inches of snow /
1 tramway / 7 chairs / Maximum rise 2,900 ft /

31 **ALTA** SKI FACTS ▶
Top station 10,550 ft / 8 chairs / 4 tows /
Good powder skiing / Maximum rise 1,300 ft /

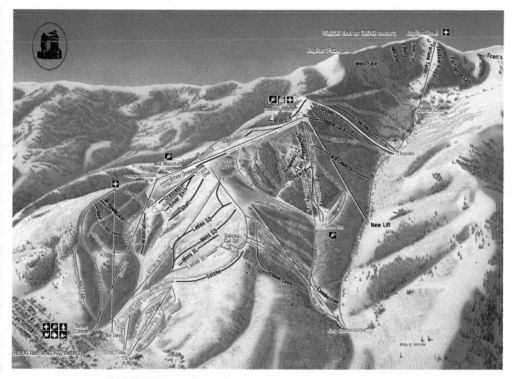

PARK CITY SKI FACTS

Top station 10,000 ft / 1 cabin /
11 chairs / Maximum rise 2,400 ft /

with live music. It has been imaginatively set in the engine room of the cablecar and the red paint and brass spokes of the massive wheel gleam at the disco dancers from behind a glass wall. There are a few essential shops in the same building, the Snowbird Center, sited round the bottom station of the tram.

Alta, just five minutes drive from Snowbird, is small in size but large in reputation among expert skiers. Here the season is longer, the runs steeper, the snow lighter and deeper than in any of the other Utah resorts. The first lift in Alta went up in the thirties and the great ambition of the regulars, who book their rooms twelve months ahead each year, is that Alta will never change. With fewer than 1,000 beds in its five lodges and two condominiums, housing is a problem. Conservation prevents further building and also limits the lifts to the existing six chairs and two tows. The whole village is compact. Lodges are built facing the main slope so it is possible to ski straight from lobby to lift. A rope tow runs conveniently between the lifts and short tows rise from it back to the lodges.

There is a beginners' area to one side and 3-mile long runs for intermediates. The High Rustler trail is long, steep and mogul-ridden, so all standards are catered for. But it is the powder that falls so frequently – often 50 inches at a time – that draws skiers back year after year to make their own tracks down their favorite slopes. Steep gullies are kept unpacked and instructors specialise in teaching how to ski down them. The Baldy Chutes are renowned for their narrow, breathtaking drops.

Après-ski is not a feature of Alta's life. Evenings are spent quietly in the hotels with an occasional visit down the road to the Tram Room at Snowbird.

A recent craze is the return of the Telemark turn. In the twenties, before bindings were developed which clamped the skiboot to the ski, long sweeping turns were made with one knee touching the ski and one heel raised. Utah's skiers are finding a new challenge in using modern crosscountry skis down the steep trails. Clamped only at the toe like skis in the twenties, they can be used for Telemark turns provided the skier has sufficient strength and delicate balance to control them.

The airport at Salt Lake City is used by several airlines. Many skiers who land there go straight by bus or taxi to their resort. Some prefer to use the City itself as a base, where the sightseeing covers the Mormon Temple, the Beehive House where the Mormon Founder lived, the colorful Trolley Square where old vehicles have been converted into a shopping and eating center, and a pioneer museum.

All this may interest the tourist but for the committed and expert skier it is the mountains around which will provide the ultimate satisfaction of challenging slopes and the driest, lightest powder of the world. Utah is for the connoisseur.

UNITED STATES OF AMERICA

Lake Tahoe

maps
pages 144,
145, 148

Northstar Kirkwood

Alpine Meadows

Squaw Valley

Heavenly Valley

A cobalt blue lake that mirrors the sparkling
white Sierra Mountains makes the setting for five major ski resorts on
the California-Nevada borders. Hundreds of thousands of westerners
from cities such as San Francisco, Los Angeles, Reno and Las Vegas
come up to enjoy the clean clear air and the snowy slopes of Northstar,
Kirkwood, Alpine Meadows, Squaw Valley and Heavenly Valley.
Everthing seems slightly larger than life in this rich playground, from
the 25 sq ft jacuzzi at Northstar to the Olympic courses at Squaw Valley,
from the Californian pines to the Nevada gaming houses.

Northstar is the perfect resort for the family with young children. Its
slopes are gentle and although there are eight lifts radiating like
fingers up 2,200 ft, all the runs from the top funnel down the small
village center, so children can set off together without the grown ups
and always find their way home.

The area is privately owned. It was once a tree nursery and Douglas
fir and Ponderosa pine still scatter the area. The guiding rule when
building has been to blend lifts, runs, parking areas and housing into
their surroundings so that they are camouflaged. Most of the
condominiums are set in gardens stocked with azaleas a mile or two
from the slopes. Shuttle buses make transport easy and many of the car
parks are small.

Ticket sales are controlled; 5,500 people are allowed on the mountain
at any one time and there is a capacity on the lifts of 10,000 an hour, so
there is no waiting about in lifts and the 19 miles of trails can be skied
again and again. Snow making insures that there are no bare patches
on the lower slopes.

Northstar boasts an excellent ski school, geared especially to
teaching children and beginners. They will look after 6-to-12 year olds

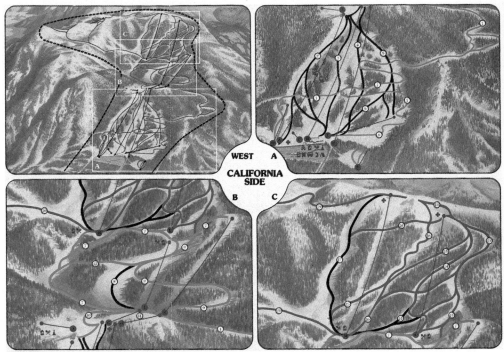

WEST A

CALIFORNIA SIDE

B C

HEAVENLY VALLEY SKI FACTS
America's largest ski resort accessible from California and Nevada /
Top station 10,040 ft / 1 Aerial tramway / 15 chairs /
3 drags and 2 mitey mites / Maximum rise 1,700 ft /

ALPINE MEADOWS SKI FACTS
Top station 8,529 ft / 13 lifts service ski terrain suitable for all grades
of skier. Lift pass interchangeable with Squaw Valley
with a one-day option for Heavenly Valley or Kirkwood /

California Lifts and Runs

Heavenly Valley Ski Area has its Main Lodge and a large paved parking area on the California side of the mountain, located just off Ski Run Boulevard in the city of South Lake Tahoe.

Lifts		Vertical	Top Elevation	Capacity Per Hour	Time (Mins.)
A	Aerial Tramway	1700	8300	400	5
B	Gunbarrel	1700	8300	1400	9
C	West Bowl	1700	8300	950	9
D	World Cup	315	6915	800	4
E	West Bowl Poma Lift	180	6800	550	3
F	Mitey Mites - for Beginners				
G	Patsy's	300	8400	750	3
H	Groove	300	8450	900	3
I	Waterfall	1000	8900	750	5
J	Pioneer Bowl Poma Lift	100	8240	250	2
K	Powder Bowl	1100	9000	900	5
L	Ridge	1000	9800	750	9
M	Sky	1500	10040	900	10

Runs

● Easiest   ■ Intermediate   ◆ Most Difficult

1	Roundabout	13	Ridge Run
6	Poma Trail	14	Betty's
7	Maggie's	15	Canyon
9	Mombo	16	Liz's
10	Patsy's	18	Ellie's Swing
11	Groove	19	Skyline Trail
12	Swing Trail	20	California Trail

2	East Bowl
3	Gunbarrel
4	Pistol
5	West Bowl
8	Waterfall
17	Ellie's

Skiers going to Nevada—Take Sky Chair and turn left to the Skyline Trail. Start your return to California by 3:15 PM.

Trail Marking and Map Legends

‼ Ski Lift	⚷ Ski Rental	⚠ Sport Shop
● Easiest	✕ Restaurant	Ⓟ Parking
■ Intermediate	🚻 Rest Room	Ⓢ Ski School
◆ Most Difficult	☎ Phone	Ⓝ Ticket Sales
▬▬ Ski Area Boundary	✚ Ski Patrol	🚌 Bus and Taxi

Please ski with caution and consideration for others. Be aware of changing conditions. Natural and man made obstacles exist. Respect closed trail and area boundary signs. They are closed for your protection. We reserve the right to revoke your ticket for reckless or out of control skiing, or for failure to observe rules and regulations.

Nevada Lifts and Runs

The Base Lodges and paved parking areas on the Nevada side are located at the top of the Kingsbury Grade (Nevada State Route 19).

Lifts		Vertical	Top Elevations	Capacity Per Hour	Time (Mins.)
A	Boulder (Lower Lift)	400	7600	950	5
B	Boulder (Upper Lift)	1400	9000	950	12
C	Wells Fargo	1600	7850	1200	8
D	Stage Coach	1500	9000	1200	12
E	East Peak	1800	9600	1200	6
F	Mitey Mites - for Beginners				
G	Dipper	1300	9900	1200	11

Runs

● Easiest   ■ Intermediate   ◆ Most Difficult

1	Edgewood	3	Olympic Downhill	2	North Bowl
5	Toiyabe Trail	4	075	9	What the Hell
		6	Stage Coach	10	Men's Downhill
		7	China Flat	11	Milky Way Bowl
		8	The Galaxy	14	Big Dipper Bowl
		12	Dipper Knob Trail	17	Little Dipper Bowl
		13	Big Dipper		
		15	Orion		
		16	Jacks		
		18	Bonanza Bowl		
		19	Skyline Trail		
		20	California Trail		
		21	$100 Saddle		
		22	East Peak Run		
		23	Ponderosa		
		24	Von Schmidt Trail		

Skiers going to California—Take Dipper Chair and turn right to the California Trail, or take East Peak Chair, turn left, go past Bonanza Bowl and enter Von Schmidt Trail. Start your return to Nevada by 3:15 PM.

Trail Marking and Map Legends

‼ Ski Lift	⚷ Ski Rental	⚠ Sport Shop
● Easiest	✕ Restaurant	Ⓟ Parking
■ Intermediate	🚻 Rest Room	Ⓢ Ski School
◆ Most Difficult	☎ Phone	Ⓝ Ticket Sales
▬▬ Ski Area Boundary	✚ Ski Patrol	🚌 Bus and Taxi
	✦ Walking	

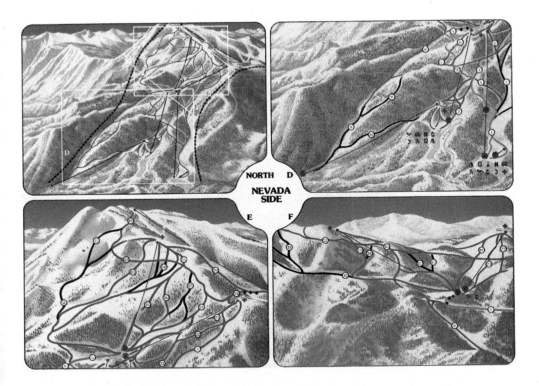

NORTH   D

NEVADA SIDE

E   F

all day. If parents want to go out at night, there are lists of babysitters at the rental office. Perhaps it is the bright Californian sunshine; perhaps it is the gentle slopes; perhaps it is the encouraging ski school; but Northstar would make a happy skier out of the most disheartened and clumsy patron.

Kirkwood, like Northstar, opened in 1972 but its history goes right back to Zachary Kirkwood who opened an old inn there in 1864. The inn is still serving meals.

The resort is tucked 30 miles back into the Sierras, far enough to be off the electric grid so that it has to generate its own power. This has limited lift expansion but the eight chairs cover a challenging range. They run in a series from the floor of the valley to points along a long ridge over head. The ridge is high, the skiing goes up to 9,800 ft and Thimble Peak, the summit, is not far short of 10,000 ft. The height catches 450 inches of snow a year and keeps it cold and dry. The steep chutes come off the ridge like funnels. Kirkwood is for the technician.

Alpine Meadows, just seven miles from Tahoe City, shows all the evidence of thoughtful planning. On the road up to the big day lodge there is just the odd glimpse of chalets among the big trees. The ski area is well kept and it is worth scheduling the day, for there is immense variety in this appealing resort.

Children can be safely handed over to the snow school, which looks after them from the age of three in a special area behind the ski school building. The best skiing starts with the first lift at 9 o'clock in the area which rises straight up from the day lodge, over North-facing slopes. Two peaks, Ward and Scott are linked by a steep ridge. Early in the day the drops are often full of snow which has fallen overnight, but an early start is needed to find them untracked.

As the sun gathers strength it is time to explore the other side of the mountain, for the Sherwood bowls on the South face are at their best around midday. The sun softens the ice off the top layer, giving smooth, easy spring snow. There is even more development to come on this side but already there is plenty of intermediate and difficult skiing. The chair lift gives a beautiful view onto the lake glinting through a frame of pines.

If the sun is really hot – and Alpine Meadows has a very long season, closing usually at the end of May – then it melts right through the crust. Once the snow becomes slushy on the South-facing slopes it is time to return to the still excellent North-facing side. Here the area below the twin peaks is lightly scattered with big trees and the meadows open up so that there is no need to be confined to trails. The whole mountainside is skiable with endlessly beguiling variations in the landscape. There are acres of it, mostly intermediate and difficult terrain, though near the base is a gently graded beginners area.

The Alpine Meadows lift pass is interchangeable with the Squaw Valley system and there is a one-day option at Heavenly Valley or Kirkwood.

It was the Winter Olympics at Squaw Valley in 1960 which gave impetus to the building of ski resorts around Lake Tahoe. Squaw is a big resort. There are 27 ski lifts covering five High Sierra peaks, and trails from 8,900 ft down to the Olympic village elevation at 6,300 ft. The

FACTS

Location
The Sierra Mountains on the California-Nevada borders, accessible to San Francisco, Los Angeles, Reno and Las Vegas. There are five resorts, all well cared for and served by lifts.

NORTHSTAR
Opened in 1972, this is a resort tailored for families; there is a good school for children and beginners, gentle slopes to 2,200 ft, and 19 miles of trails.

KIRKWOOD
Also opened in 1972, this is a resort for the ski technician. Thimble Peak rises to nearly 10,000 ft.

FACTS

ALPINE MEADOWS
Resort close to Tahoe City with great variety and a snow school for very young children. The whole mountain-side is skiable and there is skiing for all standards.

SQUAW VALLEY
The impetus for development came with the 1960 Olympics and accommodation is in the old Olympic Village. Trails drop from 8,900 ft to 6,300 ft. Suitable for poor to expert skiers.

HEAVENLY VALLEY
Largest ski area in the USA, covering 20 miles of skiable terrain. Top of the Milky Way Bowl is at 10,167 ft. Skiing for all standards. A night life of gambling, casinos, top entertainers and hotels to suit every pocket.

cablecar goes up to Granite Chief at 8,200 ft where there is a big mid station complete with restaurant, looking out across the slopes towards the lake.

In keeping with its racing tradition, Squaw Valley has some spine-chilling faces. KT22 lift goes up a slope which some unhappy skier only came down by making 22 kickturns. Generally however, the whole mountain is kept beautifully groomed, so that there is plenty of space for the poorer skier to traverse while plucking up courage for a turn. As rocks begin to come through the snow in the spring, they are painted red. Then in the summer, all the red rocks are flattened or taken out so that they don't rip the ski soles of the next year's skiers. Compared with the sheltered variety of Alpine Meadows, Squaw is big, bold and bare. Most of the trails are above the tree line and have names like Siberia, but there are sunny sheltered points like Gold Coast, where skiers sit out for lunch. Three nights a week the lights are turned on between 5 and 10 pm so that skiers can beat up and down the Searchlight and Exhibition trails.

The Olympic village remains as living quarters and the great ice arena still stands nearby. At the foot of the cablecar station, there is a rather scrappy collection of ski shops, bars and boutiques. Most visitors live at condos down near the lake and drive up every day to test their skill on the Headwall or just crisscross the web of open trails. Even expert skiers have plenty to occupy them.

Extensive as Squaw is, Heavenly Valley can boast that it is America's largest ski resort. So large, it seems, that one state cannot contain it, and it sits astride the border between Nevada and California with a ski area on either side.

Riding up in the tram on the California side, it seems that the slopes plunge straight into the lake, and looking North it is easy to see the point on the lake where California stops and Nevada starts. The low condominiums set among the trees give way abruptly to skyscrapers which house the big casinos. Many of the Nevada hotels are luxurious, such as Harrah's Tahoe Hotel, which invites stars such as Sammy Davis Junior and the Osmonds to perform.

There is no lack of more modest hotels, replete with banks of obligatory slot machines as well as the green baize tables for black jack and roulette, which make their money from gambling and charge little for rooms and food. Skiers have learned to stay on the Nevada side and drive off to the slopes by day. Ski packages include lodging, lift tickets, and complementary casino passes. The casinos also run excellent shuttle buses to the slopes and, at night, to the condominiums which lie on the California side.

There is a 4,000 ft vertical drop from the top of Heavenly to the car park and as this extends on both sides of the mountain, the resort earns its 'largest-in-America' name. The steepest slopes are near the bottom: Gunbarrel, where the first chair went up in 1955, is a steep and icy bump slope. But a second chair was put in after the boost given by the 1960 Olympics and the tram in 1962. Around the top of the tram is a plesant beginners area, where novices can enjoy being up the mountain with all the beauty of the lake below, rather than having to be content with the lower slopes. Further up are more intermediate trails

Operated under Special Use Permit, U.S. Forest Service. El Dorado National Forest

KIRKWOOD

and lifts to the boundary at the top. The Nevada side is more peaceful and as well as the blue waters of the lake there is a view of the Nevada Desert. The Galaxy run winds for seven miles from 10,167 ft at the top of the Milky Way Bowl to the base of the Wells Fargo chair at 6,100 ft. In all there's 20 square miles of skiing terrain, with an average annual snowfall of 400 inches and trails as long as seven miles.

The ski school has developed a line of teaching which they call the natural easy carve (NEC) method, which soon has skiers turning confidently. There is video, too, to highlight mistakes and help skiers analyse how to put their technique right.

The whole Lake Tahoe region shimmers like the clear water of the lake itself. Just to drive around the lakeside road, passing the deep splendor of Emerald Bay, dining out on the lake among the summer boats at Jakes on the Lake or winding through the beautifully planted gardens of the condominiums, it is easy to see why this has become the playground of the rich. The snow does not have the dry powdery texture of the Wasatch range in Utah, for the wind comes off the sea and the water content is higher, but snow does land in great quantity and the southern sun can be relied upon.

In the days of the pioneers to the Sierras between 1856 and 1876, the famous Snowshoe Thompson carried the mail through the Sierras. He trudged up the passes on his snowshoes, then strapped on his skis for the long descents. He would be surprised if he could see today what has happened to his inhospitable surroundings.

UNITED STATES OF AMERICA

Alaska

There are few ski resorts where the sea is within sight of the peaks of the skiing area. But from Chilcoot Ridge, the top of Mount Alyeska, there is a view of Turnagain Arm, the inlet where Captain Cook had to turn back when he came up against the Alaskan mountains instead of the North West Passage.

The top lift at Alyeska reaches 3,200 ft, only a quarter of the height of the Californian ski stations but the trails are snow covered well into April right down to the resort at 300 ft, so there is a respectable vertical drop. The top slopes form a big bowl of snow above the tree line, so

Mount McKinley, Alaska

that the trails and bump slopes meet at the center point. From here a chair lift takes the skier back up to try another of the bowl runs, to cut across to the Skyride restaurant, or to descend right down through the trees to resort level. There is a downhill course which has been used for the United States national championships and some easy trails, too.

Helicopter and small plane skiing are easily arranged at Alyeska. Whenever it is fine, Far North Ski Guides take groups of skiers to explore the Chugach, Kenai and Talkeetna mountains. The wilderness is impressive and the ski terrain superb. The guides are professionally trained and equipped with safety aids.

The lack of altitude at Alyeska has important effects. Although snow can be relied upon into late Spring, the weather is milder then than it is in the high Rockies of the Pacific States. The people, too, are more relaxed, quiet and self-possessed. There is a frontier feel about the way they live. Curiously there are very few Eskimo or American Indian faces; most of the people have come up from California and Oregon with the idealistic outlook of the one-time hippie who has learnt responsibility.

Juneau, a seaport to the South East is the state capital of Alaska but the main sea and air port is Anchorage, the terminal for the great pipeline which brings oil down from the wells in the far North, and a booming city. Construction workers earn huge salaries to compensate for the comparative isolation and the tough winters they have to endure. The blocks of hotels and strip clubs make Anchorage an ugly place but its shops and restaurants are crammed with good merchandise and excellent food.

Alyeska is just forty minutes drive away from Anchorage. The resort is small and from the slopes above it resembles nothing more than a huddle of wooden houses. But down in the village there is a comforting sense of solidarity and warmth. The smokey saloon in the Nugget Inn is dominated by a huge stuffed polar bear which stands above the bar. It looks down on groups of bearded drinkers in their checked wool shirts and corduroy pants who are more than capable of coping with long winter nights and Arctic temperatures. The Nugget Inn is the only hotel, though there is a row of condos close to the lower lifts and there are a couple of restaurants. The Inn's 32 rooms have their own bathrooms; there is a shop, and a restaurant.

Food in Alaska is original and fresh. Reindeer, of course, features on the menu and Alaskan King Crabs which have large succulent legs. Halibut is fished and cooked straight from the sea and there is a berry jelly which is native to the area.

Traces of the old goldrush days remain in Alyeska. There is a working goldmine a few miles from the resort which everyone is welcome to try a hand at. Jade is another precious product of Alaska and it is worked there, for all to see and buy, into jewelry which is cool and smooth to touch.

Huskies still trot round the villages, as surprisingly friendly pets. Tourists can drive a team of dogs, or simply sit back and enjoy being driven through the forest on a sled. Marathon dog sled races are common.

Crosscountry skiing is also traditional to the area and there are trails to explore around Alyeska. A beautiful course winds among great Christmas trees at Russian Jack Springs.

The days are long in April, when the sun does not start to set until 5.30. Even then it takes an hour to go down, turning the sky every color of the spectrum from deep purple to palest green as it does so.

Alaska is original. The chair lifts and air excursions make it a true ski resort but where else can a skier pan for gold; watch jade being cut and polished; drive a team of huskies and be surrounded by the relaxed warmth of people who are opening up a new frontier?

FACTS

Location	Ski resort	Accommodation	Activities
Mount Alyeska, 40 miles from the Anchorage, in the far North East corner of the State.	The village of Alyeska serves Chilcoot Range. Altitudes are only from 300 ft to 3,200 ft but there is snow until April. There is cross-country skiing to Chugach, Kenai, Talkeetna and a trail to Russian Jack Springs. The wilderness is impressive and the ski terrain superb.	In this small village, there are some condominiums and an inn. Any night life is at the inn.	Gold mining for the tourist, buying jade, driving a dog sleigh, watching dog sled racing, heliskiing.

UNITED STATES OF AMERICA

Colorado

Vail   Beaver Creek
Winter Park   Aspen
Copper Mountain

maps
pages
156–157

Colorado's great peaks and forested valleys are studded with ski resorts. Most of the land is owned by the US Forestry Service and conservation is preached – and observed – in every valley. It has not stopped superb ski areas being opened to thousands of skiers. They fly in from all over the country to Denver's mile-high city and from there pick up a rental car to drive to one of the thirty resorts. From Arapahoe East with three lifts to the Aspen mountain quartet of Ajax, Highlands, Buttermilk and Snowmass with 32 lifts, from Berthoud Pass where the first lift was built in 1937 to Beaver Creek which opened in 1981, there is tremendous variety in Colorado skiing right down through the alphabet of resorts to the sophistication of Vail and the casual family atmosphere of Wolf Creek.

Vail's mountain is the greatest in the state. In ten square miles of ski terrain there are trails up to $4\frac{1}{2}$ miles long and a total of 57 miles of prepared skiing. Tyros and tigers can set off together from many of the peaks: the unsteady following winding easy trails and the adventurous hurtling down the more direct bump slopes. As the trails cross there's the advantage that they meet from time to time as they cover the mountain in their separate ways.

In addition to the front face of the mountain, Vail's great glory hides on the other side, where the Back Bowls lie. Over a century ago during warfare between Indians from the plains and those from the mountains, a great tract of forest was burned down. As water is scarce in the uplands, the trees have been slow to grow again, and this has opened up two great bowls which are frequently dredged overnight with light powder. Enthusiastic skiers crowd the earliest lift to make their own tracks down the steep slopes. Entry to the bowl is controlled; special gates channel the skiers at first to avoid avalanche danger but, once through, the skiers are free to take off among the sparse trees. Down at the bottom the bowls meet and a chair lift leads back again to the top – where many set off again for another plunge into the waist-high powder.

previous page
**Cimarron
River,
Colorado**

Down in Vail the main village stretches along two miles of valley. Intermediates take the long Lionshead gondola in the East; experts go up the Golden Peak chair from West Vail, and to spread the crowds and give variety there are three other chair lifts rising from the village. Even so, lift lines build up at high season, though Vail limits the number of passes sold. On either side of the main town, the condominiums stretch out along the valley for ten miles or more, providing beds for 16,000.

The efficiency of the mountain layout is mirrored in the village below. Tennis, swimming, skating and racquets are all waiting when the skier comes off the slopes and a shuttle bus travels round and round picking up and dropping passengers. A feature of the night life is the chain of pedestrianized squares full of stores and restaurants. There are piano rooms and Italian trattorias, French Cuisine, pizzas and pasta, steaks, seafood and hamburgers. Mexican tacos and tortillas are specially good at Los Amigos or outside town at the Saloon at Minturn. Vail is no two-day resort. The range of its slopes and the entertainment are sufficient to keep all but the most demanding skier happy for a two-week vacation.

Beaver Creek was planned when Denver put in to host the 1976 Olympics, but Denver withdrew after being awarded the Games, which eventually took place in Innsbruck. As a result the development of Beaver Creek hung fire. Now after five years more planning, it is open.

Respect for the environment is the keynote to the development. There is accommodation for only 9,000 people, and the lifts can take no more than 10,000. The style of architecture is rustic and windows of the mountain lodges look onto the South sides only, to conserve heat. Islands of trees have been left in the trails. They break up what would otherwise be great gashes cut down the mountain sides, preserve the snow and improve the visibility in bad weather. Whenever snow gets scarce the snow guns are turned on in the night as the temperature drops, to make big mounds of snow to be farmed out across the pistes wherever it is needed. The generator has been sited way up the mountain so that the noise does not disturb sleepers in the condominiums below.

Everything that has been learned about cutting trails, designing lift systems and planning accommodation has gone into the building of Beaver Creek. Ex-President Gerald Ford, for long a visitor to Vail, was one of the first to buy a plot. In this area celebrities are so common that they do not get stared at when they want to relax on vacation. Beaver Creek may be expensive but it is very, very special.

Winter Park is one of the longest established resorts in the United States. When the Denver and Rio Grande railroad was being built in the 1920's, the Moffat Tunnel was cut 67 miles West of Denver and construction workers found the snow five feet deeper at the West Portal. Denverites soon found the snow too, and as the construction workers moved on, the skiers took over their huts. Gradually a resort built up and today lifts spread over two mountains – there is a third ready for development – and link Winter Park to a second resort, Mary Jane, in the next valley.

Winter Park is run by an independent company which has the

▲ **VAIL** SKI FACTS
Top station 11,250 ft / 1 cabin / 16 chairs /
1 drag / Snowmaking facilities /

▲ **COPPER MOUNTAIN** SKI FACTS
Top station 12,050 ft / 10 chairs / 1 drag /
1 mighty mite / Snowmaking facilities /

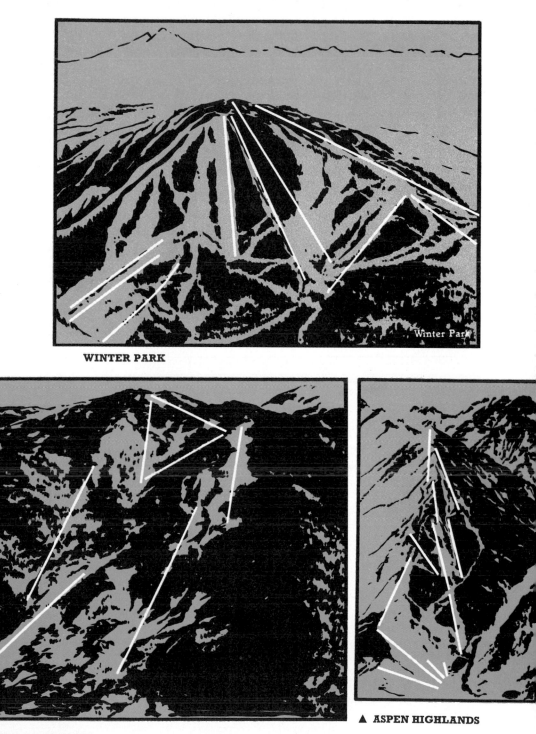

WINTER PARK

▲ **ASPEN HIGHLANDS**

ASPEN MOUNTAIN
ASPEN SKI FACTS Top station 11,800 ft / 8 chairs / 4 drags / All grades / Snowmaking facilities /

freedom to develop as it wishes, without being subject to the United States forestry laws. The railway still runs, bringing skiers in from Denver at the weekend. The area opens early in the season, usually mid-November, with the help of snowmaking, and there are 52 trails officially marked as 24% easiest; 39% more difficult; 37% most difficult. About five minutes from the West Portal, which now lies at the foot of the lift area, is the village. It caters well for families with comfortable condominiums set among the trees, and its prices are very reasonable.

Eleven double and two triple chairs keep skiers moving fast around the mountains with a vertical drop of 2,125 ft. Some of the runs are fearsome – like Drunken Frenchmen (named after the construction workers, not the tourists) but there are gentler alternatives and a whole range that is named after Alice in Wonderland so the young reader can explore Cheshire Cat, White Rabbit, Mock Turtle and Tweedle Dee.

Winter Park has an excellent ski school, which teaches children, beginners and experts up to racing standard. The Winter Park Pro team have often won the annual world pro skiing area competition. But a separate and even larger staff of ski teachers specialize in instructing handicapped skiers. The bright orange jackets of blind skiers are a familiar sight on the slopes, as well as one-legged or armless skiers, whose control of their skis is breathtaking to watch.

In keeping with its family atmosphere, Winter Park and Mary Jane have their own zany festivals, including the Spring Splash which ends the season. Skiers, in startling but suitably expendable clothes, leap off a jump, hoping to land on the other side of a pool of slushy water. The noisy failures are frequent, to the general entertainment of all the spectators.

Another resort with a family atmosphere is Copper Mountain, about the same distance from Denver as Winter Park but further North. Copper has its lifts neatly sorted alphabetically and according to difficulty. Lift A at the eastern end serves trails where the names such as Formidable, Treble Cliff and Two Much warn they are difficult. But the five main chairs rising from along the bottom edge of the mountain lead to progressively easier slopes, so that intermediate skiers will feel at home on trails from C lift, and off H chair are Care Free and Easy Feelin' trails until the wide circle of Roundabout is reached. This curious trick of mountain formation is useful in keeping expert skiers and beginners apart so that they do not get in each others' way. Bombers can bomb down from A and B chairs; amblers can amble down H and I.

Only two of Colorado's resorts, Arapahoe and Loveland Basin, go higher than Copper Mountain's 12,050 ft top elevation but even Copper Mountain keeps snow guns on several of its lower slopes. This enables the resort to start the season as early as the first week in November and finish late in April. It is an exciting place to ski. Gradually the village is building up to provide après-ski facilities. There is a Club Méditerranée, and most of the accommodation and shops are contained in a few big buildings.

Aspen is not one resort but four; it has a long history and plenty of turn-of-the-century character. It is famous for its music festivals and is the goal of every serious American skier.

FACTS

Location
To the immediate East of the Utah mountains are the Colorado ranges from Arapahoe East to the Aspen mountain, all within a short drive of Denver. The area has 30 resorts.

VAIL
Ten square miles of ski terrain, suitable for tyros and tigers; 57 miles of prepared skiing, served by a village with 16,000 beds, restaurants of several nationalities, piano rooms, and tennis, swimming, racquets and skating. 18 lifts, mainly chairs.

BEAVER CREEK
Expensive, beau tiful and exclusiv resort begun in 1976, brilliantly planned with accommodation limited to 9,000 beds.

WINTER PARK
Family resort which developed in the 1920s; excellent school for children, the blind and the physically handicapped; accommodation in family con dominiums; runs graded by diffi culty, from the fearsome Drun ken Frenchman to a range devoted to the

FACTS

young with names taken from Alice in Wonderland. Like the resort in the next valley to which it is linked, Mary Jane, it runs a series of zany festivals.

COPPER MOUNTAIN

Resort with family atmosphere, North of Winter Park and Denver, where the lifts are graded by difficulty. Runs are identified by names such as Care Free, Easy Feelin', Treble Cliff and Two Much. Maximum altitude is 12,050 ft. Good après ski is under development. 12 lifts offer excellent skiing for intermediates and advanced skiers.

ASPEN

Premier resort for skiers of all standards who regard their skiing seriously. Begun at the turn of the century and developed heavily since World War II, it has four mountains and four resorts each suited to different standards: Aspen Mountain, or Ajax, Aspen Highlands, Buttermilk and Snowmass. Good restaurants and a brilliant cultural and musical life.

There was skiing in Aspen in 1897, when silver mining prospectors went into Roaring Fork Valley, but soon after the whole area started a decline which did not end until after the Second World War. The skiing potential was developed at the same time as Walter Paepcke, a Chicago industrialist brought musicians to Aspen. Sport and culture have existed happily alongside ever since. Aspen's four mountains and four villages cover a vast area. Aspen Mountain is more commonly known as Ajax and has seven chairs. Aspen Highlands, a couple of miles away has 8. Buttermilk, developed especially for beginners and intermediates, has 5 chairs, and Snowmass 12. All form part of an integrated ski lift complex, so that the trails go satisfyingly on and on.

Aspen town is laid out in neat blocks, recalling its ancient history, and the population (after the big decline when no new building went up between 1900 and 1945) is now back above 10,000. Conservationists wanting to preserve the old-town atmosphere managed to get a ban put on building in the late 70's with the result that real estate prices soared and it is now so expensive to find a room in the town that wages have to be high too and that brings up prices for everything. There are several fine restaurants. Aspen Meadows offers *nouvelle cuisine*; Little Nell's bar is the in-place for a drink after skiing, though The Tippler at the Copper Kettle is bidding to take over with an oyster bar and dancing on the copper floor.

Despite all Aspen's elegance and culture, it is the skiing over Aspen's great slopes that is the real draw. One of the pleasures of life is to take Ruthie's Run down to the town. Lower Ruthies has a mogul slope that is steep at the sides, gentler in the middle, so it is just the place for a last descent of the day, to get a feeling of accomplishment without too much daring.

Colorado is ski country. With its great mountain ranges, abundant light snow, and easy communications, it has built up a reputation as a holiday ground for skiers.

Ski glossary

TECHNIQUE

Christiania legere Was a French method of turning, which kept the shoulders parallel with the hips so that they swung round in a turn.

Counter Rotation A technique for turning which kept the skier's shoulders facing squarely down the mountain while knees and hips twisted from side to side.

Graduated Length Method Almost identical method of ski teaching to 'ski evolutif', invented at the same time by Clif Taylor in America.

Kickturn A method of changing direction when *not* moving forward. The skier raises one ski vertically so that it rests on its tail and swings it outwards and right round until it is parallel to the other but facing in the opposite direction. The second ski is then brought round parallel with the first.

Moguls Bumps formed by hundreds of skiers turning down a steep slope and cutting channels through the snow. The word derives from the Viennese dialect word for hump – *Mogl*.

Ski Evolutif A method of teaching skiing invented by Robert Blanc of France in the 60s. The beginner was put onto skis just three feet long and, once confidence had been gained, went on to skis $4\frac{1}{2}$ ft long and so gradually longer until normal length was reached.

Schuss Going straight down a slope.

MORE SKI LANGUAGE

Gondola An enclosed chair lift in German speaking resorts: called a *telecabine* in France, an *ovovia* in Italy.

Poma A type of lift invented by Frenchman Pomagalski. A round plate hangs from a pole, which in turn is pulled up by the cable. The skier puts the plate between his legs, leans back and is pulled uphill by it.

Snowcats Machines which flatten the pistes.